Robert and Many Other Special People

ROBERT AND MANY OTHER SPECIAL PEOPLE

A Tribute to the Many People I Have Been Honored to Know Who Possess Developmental Disabilities

Joseph B. Frederick Ph.D.

Volume 3

Copyright © 2023 by Joseph B. Frederick Ph.D.

Library of Congress Control Number:		2023916276
ISBN:	Hardcover	979-8-3694-0622-9
	Softcover	979-8-3694-0621-2
	eBook	979-8-3694-0620-5

All rights reserved. No part of this book may be reproduced or transmitted in any form or by any means, electronic or mechanical, including photocopying, recording, or by any information storage and retrieval system, without permission in writing from the copyright owner.

Any people depicted in stock imagery provided by Getty Images are models, and such images are being used for illustrative purposes only. Certain stock imagery © Getty Images.

Print information available on the last page.

Rev. date: 09/07/2023

To order additional copies of this book, contact:
Xlibris
844-714-8691
www.Xlibris.com
Orders@Xlibris.com
848850

This book is dedicated to and written with respect in memory of Robert and many other special persons.

CONTENTS

Preface xi

Acknowledgments xiii

Introduction and Overview xv

PART I: The First Years of Employment in the County Board of Mental Retardation

Chapter 1   Richland County Board of Mental Retardation 1

This is about my first years of employment as a physical education teacher and recreation coordinator of children and adults (1967–1969).

Chapter 2   Lucas County Special Services Coordinator 9

My challenges as a special services coordinator, classroom consultant, and teacher were many; but the special people I knew made it worthwhile.

Chapter 3   The Early Years of Our Sons, Joe and Mark 30

Joe is the first born.

Mark was to follow.

Part II: Moving My Workplace from the County to the State Government

Chapter 4 Educational Consultant Serving Nineteen Counties in Northwest Ohio 35

This position afforded me the opportunity to encounter boards, CEOs, managers, teachers, workshop specialists, social workers, parents, and community organizations (1973–1976); but I enjoyed more my contacts with the people we served.

Chapter 5 District Manager and Other Positions 40

I was introduced to budget restrictions by having five positions of responsibility with the State Department as well as lawsuits, an $8.2 million construction project, and overseeing several million dollars of state grants for various schools, workshops, and residential projects. The office was being abolished while I was involved with many of these projects (1975–1979). All these positions helped me appreciate the people whose lives we were trying to help improve.

Chapter 6 Northwest Ohio Developmental Center 56

The staff experienced a Medicaid survey and decertification, reorganization of service delivery system, and disappearance of a resident, which looked like a kidnapping, to name a few events (1978–1981).

Chapter 7 Regional Commissioner 61

Several group homes were established and opened in Northwest Ohio while the regional offices were being abolished (1981–1983). This allowed many people to return to their community.

Chapter 8 Impact Grants Coordinator..69

I started a new state incentive in which program funding was made available to all eighty-eight counties in the state for any person leaving a state developmental center (1983–1985). These grants helped cover costs in the community.

Chapter 9 Chief of State Case Management..72

I oversaw the process of transferring the case management positions from the state to the county system (1985). This put the supervision of people services at the county level.

Part III: A Second and Third Chance with the County and Bowling Green State University (BGSU)

Chapter 10 Wood County Director of Day Services and Director of Special Projects..79

In Bowling Green, Ohio, among other duties, I was a major factor in the establishment of a Wood County fuel center, was responsible for overall supervision, and worked for continued positive changes in the Wood Lane School, Wood Lane Industries maintenance department, Special Olympics, volunteers, public relations, and transportation department (1985–2001). This gave better services by having people work for needed changes.

Chapter 11 The Doctoral Degree and Teaching at BGSU..................92

The use of consumers in my classes was twofold. It gave the consumers a chance to talk about the advancements in their lives, and it gave students firsthand experiences with these great consumers.

Chapter 12   Henry County Board of Developmental Disabilities 95

It was budget needs and new federal waivers for income in a county with many consumer needs (2000–2006).

PART IV: Retirement Experience

Chapter 13   Retirement Years 103

Here are more special people I have known

PREFACE

Each of us lives our life according to our heredity, living circumstances, and exposure to other people. In my book, *People + Me*, I covered my background in a small railroad town in Northern Ohio named Willard. The feedback I received from this book was more positive than I could have imagined. People continued to ask me, "When will the next book be printed?"

As I reviewed the information that I had collected and the first draft I had written on the second book, I decided to go forward with another book. The title came easy. As I looked at my professional career and my personal life at that time, it was evident that *God Keeps On Giving* me many blessings.

Once again, people asked me when I was going to write another book. Like my other books, this book, *Robert and Many Other Special People*, is filled with events that I think others will find interesting. I was inspired to write this book after reading *Petey*, a book written by Ben Mikaelson about a person with developmental disabilities and other handicaps. I felt called to pay tribute to many of these people I knew who had influenced my life. I hope you enjoy reading and honoring all these people I now present.

Acknowledgments

I have always appreciated the support of my extremely caring and loving wife, Kathy, in the time I gave to writing and editing this book for content and other factors. I appreciate the support of my sons, Mark, and Joe II; my daughter-in-law, Tara; and my grandsons, Josh and Zach, as well as my family and friends for allowing me to write about them.

God's gift of life to me is the supreme acknowledgment. My life is really God's life, and my goal is to always use these blessings and gifts to His honor and glory through this book.

Again, I wish to give recognition to Jamie Welty for his excellent skills in accomplishing the comprehensive editing of this book and giving helpful suggestions in its content. Without Jamie's and Kathy's suggestions, this book would not have been possible. The cover was made possible by my good friend Denny Walston, who is always able to do wonders with photography. Special thanks to Liz Sheets for her contributions.

In addition, I acknowledge the many special people who have shared with me and continue to share with me their lives. I have gained more from them about how to live life and enjoy it to the fullest than I could ever give back to these people who are more like us than I or they will ever know. Thank You.

This book would not have been possible if it had not been for my publisher, Xlibris. Mary Flores worked with me through the entire process, and I owe much to her hard work. A special thank you to May Arado, Emman Villaran and Harriet Fulton for the essential final touches. The staff supported my every need to make this book the best it could be.

I must thank Gene Walston's wife, Ellen, for giving me permission to use his picture with Robert as the cover. We were headed to Michigan with my wife, Kathy, when I said to Ellen, "I would love to use Gene's picture with Robert (on the right) as the cover for the book." Ellen said, "That would be OK." I was elated. It took us several months to find the cover picture, and I thank God we did.

Introduction and Overview

About the Direction and Title

The direction of this book is to cover the years I spent in the world of work and my associated private life at that time. To say that my years working in my career were enjoyable and challenging would be an understatement. My private life was also enjoyable and challenging. My life in these years was in many ways a mystery. As you read, you will see many eventful happenings and energy whose base was my God and Savior. It is my hope that *Robert and Many Other Special People* will be a book as good as the books *People + Me* and *God Keeps On Giving*.

The Influence of Others on Me

This book is about people in my life with developmental disabilities. As time passed, another thought about the title of my book struck me. I am but a product of all my experiences, which include all other people, if I am open to them. It works another way. Other people who are open to me would have the capability of showing reflections of me in their lives. We are all more like others than different when we analyze their influence on our lives and ours on theirs.

Our influences on others and theirs on us are at times recognized. Often, influences are not recognized, but they do take place. The importance of influences is that they do take place and are often helpful to others, not that people get credit. In these writings, recognition for helpful actions is many times an incomplete act.

Goals

Knowing and getting to where one wishes to be in life is of paramount importance. That is why my life has been driven by goals. I would speculate that some of my major goals are like many of your goals: to love God, to obtain an education, to have meaningful relationships, to fall in love, to marry, to have children, and to be successful at one's profession. In the end, we hope to find sources of fulfillment and happiness. One other more unusual goal for me was to write this book based on my experiences. All goals had one common denominator: to help me live a worthwhile existence and, if possible, in the process, help other people on their life journeys.

Support

In pursuing my goals, I have realized that other people often supported me even when I thought I was trying to help them. Over the years, I have found, and it will be evident as you read, that the greatest help I have received was from God. I feel my twin who died at three months in utero has been another important influence on me.

Writing the Book

As I have grown older and experienced various events, I made it a practice to constantly document and share the many good and not-so-positive times in my life. The passing of people, particularly my father, mother, sister, and especially my son Mark, as well as many friends and neighbors, has always caused me to think about life's journey. My hope is that I can pay homage to the many people and the most influential being in my life, God. When I have a potentially noticeable experience, either in the present or in the past, I tried to quickly evaluate the happening to see if it is one that I can document and share. It is exciting for me to have the opportunity to share my life and the people in my life with others. It is more than exciting; it is a major driving force in my life to develop this book for others' enjoyment and benefit. While it is impossible to sum up one's life in a book, it is possible to leave behind stories about many other wonderful people and myself.

It was never my intention to embarrass, make fun of, or in any way put down anyone in my writings. If I made an error in judgment and hurt someone, I am sorry. You see, writing this book is a risk. The risk is that, at times, I may not convey the information in the best possible manner; and it would be offensive. To guard against this possibility, I have obtained permission from others when appropriate. While at times I used the involved individuals' real names, other times I did not.

In writing this book, I have striven to make the text interesting, the contents related to the readers' needs; entertaining yet not dragging on; and one that can be read in either short or long periods with the use of vignettes. In the attempt to make the book interesting, I have tried to describe the many individuals in as much detail as possible. Race, color, and creed where appropriate are included. Since most people are of the color of white, I did not describe these individuals as such. Afro-American, Hispanic, and others were described as it added to the text; and I wished to honor their natural makeup. It is important that the text be understood by the intended audience and that the content has some commonality with the readers' lives. I ask you to enjoy the readings and forgive any unintentional errors in the text.

Experiences in our lives are unique to each of us. No other person can go through them as we have. Yet experiences do usually have similarities with other people. For example, when we were into the Halloween holiday, we had the anticipation of obtaining lots of candies. We were also into choosing the right costume and going with our siblings or friend's door to door in the neighborhood. When we hear, see, think, or read about Halloween, we identify with these memories. As you read this book, my hope is that you can identify with many of the experiences I have gone through and enjoy parts of your life again.

One Book Becomes Three

I invite you to join me in reliving my life experiences and important lessons I have learned from them. As I began writing the book, the number of pages dictated that two books must be the result. The first volume covers my life from the beginning up to and including my first year of marriage and is titled *People + Me*. The second volume covers my professional career and exemplifies, as the title states, that *God Keeps On Giving* to me professionally and personally. The third volume is *Robert and Many Other Special People* covering many of the special people I have had the honor of knowing.

Influence of Others

Many people have made a difference in my life. I have seen that everyone I have known or will meet may potentially affect my life in some way. A poem sent to me for Christmas in 2007 by Maxine Mobley, grandmother to my daughter-in-law, Tara, written by an unknown author, captured my sentiments on the influence of other people affecting my life very accurately. Part of the poem went like this:

For I am but a total of the many folks I've met
And you happen to be one of those I prefer never to forget,
And whether I have known you for many years or few,
In some way you have had a part of shaping things I do.

Everyone's life is shaped by others. Please enjoy how mine has been shaped by the special people in my life and possibly by you.

PART I

The First Years of Employment in the County Board of Mental Retardation

Chapter 1

Richland County Board of Mental Retardation

Director of Physical Development and Recreation

My first association with a person with disabilities was in my hometown of Willard. A man who attended my church, St. Francis Xavier, was Gene Hines. Gene was blind from birth, but he was a very upbeat person and fun to be around. Gene lived with his mother and father, Emma, and Steve. He was a weaver making mainly rugs. People would save their cloth material; and Gene would cut them in strips, sew them together, and weave rugs. I believe other people would help make the balls of stripped cloth that were used to weave the beautiful rugs. Gene provided me with a very good model of a successfully employed person with disabilities.

Years later, I was to manage the Willard Pool and allowed a group of people with mental retardation and developmental disabilities to use the pool.

My first full-time job was physical education and recreation director. The enrollment in the school and workshop was around two hundred people. The center was one of eighty-eight county programs in the state of Ohio, which served persons with mental retardation and developmental disabilities. Simply put, the programs served individuals with mental retardation or significant subaverage general intellectual functioning existing concurrently with and demonstrated through deficits in adaptive behavior. Adaptive behavior includes the ability to communicate, travel around the community, prepare meals, and more. These deficits are manifested during the developmental period. These adaptive behaviors are essential for us to be able to live out our daily lives.

While people with mental retardation and developmental disabilities could have mental illness involvement, their primary diagnosis was usually mental retardation and developmental disabilities. Mental retardation is a very large subdivision of developmental disabilities. Developmental disabilities is a more broad term and includes areas such as cerebral palsy, epilepsy, or autism. These conditions are in some cases closely related to mental retardation and may be eligible for services under the programs offered in Ohio, eventually called the county boards of developmental disabilities. These guidelines depend on being a substantial handicap in areas of significant deficits. The condition originated before the age of eighteen and can be expected to continue indefinitely. Mental illness involves a person who is having difficulty in dealing with reality.

The superintendent of the program was Steve Woitovich. Steve had begun his career as did I as a physical development specialist. Unlike me, Steve had an educational experience in this area and shared all his vast knowledge and written documents with me. He also inspired me to write material for state and national publications. Kathy and my friends Bill and Rachel Daniels were to without any pay provide the photographs that were used in these many publications to honor the individuals I was to have the pleasure of sharing my time and God-given talents.

Once again, this position gave me the opportunity to continue to fulfill my promise to God that I had made at John Carroll University. That promise was to give back to God somehow and service other human beings for the support He gave in helping me attain a college education. While this promise was not something that had to be repaid immediately upon graduation, it was nice to get an early start.

Swimming with Billy

A new student was a young man in his teens who had not been in school previously. He came to school with his two cap guns and proceeded to tell everyone in jest he was going to shoot them. He soon left his guns at home and settled into the school schedule. Billy's disability was Down syndrome, a disability usually caused by abnormal genetic development.

Richland Newhope Center used the local YWCA pool for its swimming lessons. I had developed check sheets for each student and asked the teachers to help me keep them updated. Instruction started with blowing bubbles and could lead to swimming.

After instructing a few students, I noticed one of the newer students, Billy, approaching me from behind. Billy was about sixteen years old and was one of the largest and strongest people in the school. He had always been a very happy person and constantly had the biggest smile in the world. Before I could respond to Billy's movement, I noticed that he had put his massive arms around me and was pushing me under the water. I lost my footing and was completely under the water. I couldn't scream and was not able to breathe. As they say, my life flashed in front of me.

Since I had taken lifesaving as well as swimming for my Eagle Scout award at the Willard Pool, I had one option to put in place. Since there was no help close to me as probably nobody knew that I was drowning, I immediately swung both of my arms to the side and tried to contact the side of Billy's body to prompt the action of him loosening his bear hug. Thank God I was successful as his grip loosened, and I broke free. I don't think Billy knew that he was hurting me. After that experience, I was more aware of my surroundings especially in the pool and probably other circumstances.

Primary Age Students

There were about ten or so students in the primary class. One was a beautiful Down syndrome girl named Crystal. We had asked her mother if she could stay at our house for an evening. She agreed, and we planned a nice evening for all of us. This was a great experience for us as we learned very fast that we had to keep our eye on this energetic girl during all her waking hours. She was curious and was into many things all evening. It was an enjoyable and educative evening for us.

Two other children in the class were also beautiful children, which is many times characteristic of autistic children. Theresa was a tall thin girl who had little speech but was an excellent student. Ricky was a much shorter redhead and had little speech. This was a good introduction to me about how smart a student could be even with little ability to communicate verbally.

Boy Scouts from Richland Newhope School

While living in Mansfield, I had the good fortune to start a Boy Scout troop for the developmentally disabled. Several parents assisted me on various outings with the troop. Some of the boys did not have rides to the evening meetings, so I would pick them up on my way to the meetings. On one occasion, I was to pick up one of the scouts by the name of Bill. This tall thin boy was my first pickup, so I had gone up to the house and knocked on the door to tell them I was ready to pick up the scout. I was invited in as the boy was not yet ready. As I walked in the door, I noticed that the scout's three sisters were at the house. Shortly after I went into the house, I heard some people coming in the house. These people turned out to be the husbands of the three sisters. As the men walked in, I saw them stop dead in their tracks and look at me. I felt out of place being in the house with the three sisters. I had to think fast so I could properly tell them why I was there. Without thinking, I shouted out that I was the scoutmaster of the boy's troop. Within a split second, the men proceeded to go about their business and leave me to my own business. The scout was ready to leave, and I was also very ready to get out of the house. I often wondered what would have happened to me if I hadn't well explained to the husbands why I was in the house with their wives.

One of the boy's clothes looked like they were hand-me-downs. Whenever I would make small talk with him about his life, he would add that he had just finished a supper of "beans." I couldn't imagine what it must have been like to have beans for many of my meals.

Another one of the scouts I picked up was Delbert. Delbert was a stout teenager and was very proud of his Boy Scout uniform. I never saw a father, but his mother was a very caring person. Delbert had a habit of rolling his eyes when he was excited to talk to me, and they kind of danced. It's amazing to think of the things that were different but attractive about these special people.

Another boy in the troop was Norman. Norman was an attractive boy, curly haired, extremely well-mannered, and athletic. For one of my class projects, I was to do a case study on a person with disabilities. Norman's mother was very cooperative on this study and shared that during birth, the umbilical cord had wrapped around his head and cut off the supply of oxygen.

I really enjoyed being the leader of the troop and working with the boys. I was to leave my job at the Richland Newhope School after two years of service. Unfortunately, due to my inability to train a new scoutmaster, there was no one who took my place; so, I was afraid the troop might have died.

More about Some of the Students

I have been fascinated by the many socioeconomic backgrounds of the parents and their ability to cooperate in obtaining the best possible for their sons and daughters in the various programs I have been involved in. It has been rare, if never, that I had needed something and had not been able to find it.

For example, Michael's father was a medical doctor. At times, his parents had wanted to go out for the evening, and they needed a guardian for the evening. Kathy and I were more than happy to volunteer. We enjoyed being with Mike and enjoyed the extra money. After the board meetings, we would go to the Wood Street Cafe and have a drink. Michael's father was on the board and would always have a split of champagne. It was a good board and a great first professional job. I was taking a course at BGSU at the time on mental retardation. One of the chapters was on Down syndrome, and I learned the different types of this classification. When I mentioned Mike's type of syndrome one day to his father, he asked me how I knew this, and I said I had learned it in my studies. He was very impressed with this bit of information that I knew.

Another student was Jackie. Jackie's father was in some type of business, and he was also one of the men who would go on campouts with the Boy Scouts. Jackie was a large young girl and was a person with Down syndrome. I was always impressed with her ability to balance on the trampoline.

Mark was another student, and his father was in insurance and very active in the parents' association. Mark tended to be present when things were going a little off course. He also was a person with Down syndrome. Mark enjoyed scouts and had very red hair.

Another of the school children was Yolanda. She was a very thin and athletic African American girl. She could do about any trick on the trampoline, loved to dance, and played a good game of basketball.

John was a teenager, and his father was superintendent of one of the local schools. John always had a smile on his face. John was also a person with Down syndrome and enjoyed physical education.

A second boy named Mark was always cheerful. He was a teenager, and his father was in the loan business. Mark enjoyed scouts and was always up for gym class. His mother was very active in the parents' association and a treat to work with on projects.

Adults in the Sheltered Workshop

In the summer of 1968, there was an opening to run the sheltered workshop. I applied and received the position. While there were few adults at that time who worked in the community, I enjoyed the opportunity to run the workshop.

One of the adults who worked there was Kenny. Kenny was a person with cerebral palsy. Kenny had a three-wheel bike and rode it every day that he could to work. One of the jobs we had was to tear apart old electric meters, and the workshop sold the scrap metal. Wages were determined on how many meters were disassembled. Despite Kenny's physical disabilities, he was able to disassemble the meters faster than any other employee, and he really enjoyed his work.

Another employee in the workshop was Big John. John was very tall and loved to play basketball. John was African American and always had a big smile for you.

The Move Is On

The completion of my master's degree was foremost in my mind, and the two-hour drive to and from BGSU was demanding. Leaving after school and getting home around one o'clock the next morning took its toll on my sleep. While I enjoyed the company of two other men both named

Bob on the drive, I knew I could not finish my degree commuting from Mansfield.

A job advancement at the Lucas County Board of Mental Retardation and Developmental Disabilities in Toledo, Ohio, made a move possible. It was goodbye to the many good people in the Mansfield area.

CHAPTER 2

Lucas County Special Services Coordinator

We moved to Wood County to attend BGSU and work in the Lucas County Board of Mental Retardation and Developmental Disabilities in Toledo. Kathy and I were both enrolled in BGSU. My new job was director of physical education and recreation. This was a new job in Lucas County. My job in Richland County was also a new position with me being the first person to fill the job. Mary Bradberry, a state program consultant, had taken me under her wing; and she encouraged me to interview for the job. Since I needed a job near BGSU, I requested an interview. I always had the idea that Mary had put in a good word for me.

Interview with Walt

My interview was scheduled for late in the day as I was traveling from Mansfield to Toledo. As we approached the Larc Lane School in South Toledo, I noticed another person leaving their car. The gentleman came over to the car and said, "Who are you trying to find?" I said, "I am looking for Mr. Solarz, the superintendent." He told me he was Walt Solarz and invited me into the building. I introduced myself and my wife, Kathy. As I began getting out of the car, he asked Kathy if she was going to one of the local malls. She explained that she didn't know the area and would just wait in the car. He invited Kathy to come into the building rather than staying in the car. He told Kathy she could be part of the interview process. I liked this guy immediately and was to learn much from him.

The interview was one of the most enjoyable interviews I had ever experienced. Walt felt comfortable that I was the man for the position. At this point in the interview, he asked Kathy if she had plans to work. Kathy explained that she was a nurse and would be looking for work. Since we only had one car, Kathy would need to find a place of employment that I could drop her off in the morning and pick her up at night. Walt explained that he had a position open in the school that would be available to Kathy if she was interested. Kathy had always believed the old saying, "A bird in the hand is worth two in the bush." We had a very profitable meeting that day as both Kathy and I had obtained jobs before moving to Wood County. Both Kathy and I were to have a very long and positive relationship with Walt and the staff.

Finding a New Home Near Bowling Green, Ohio

Kathy and I had less than a month to find a dwelling near Bowling Green. I was to start graduate summer school in June on a federal grant program, and we had two weekends to find a rental property. The first weekend, we didn't find anything we liked. We went up on a Friday night of the last weekend we had to find a rental and stayed with friends of ours, Bob and Cathi Schodorf. We went to bed at a respectable time, but one of the apartment neighbors had decided to burn trash. We shut the window, but once smoke is inside, it will not leave.

We got a few hours' sleep and woke up very early on Saturday morning to look for a newspaper that would carry area rental housing listings. We were standing in downtown Maumee and saw a newspaper container that was empty. We figured the delivery truck would be coming shortly. We were correct. The papers came off the truck, and we gave the correct change and took the newly printed paper. There was one ad that caught our attention. It was a home in the country, and the price was right. We called the number on a pay phone and talked to the owner. He said he had other calls, but we were welcome to come out. It took us less than fifteen minutes to get out to the home.

We met the landlord and saw the house. The house was small yet large enough for us. The first floor had a bedroom, a bathroom, a kitchen, and a living room. There were two bedrooms upstairs and a full basement. The house was painted white, and there was a block building behind the house for two cars. We said we would take the house. It seems there is almost always a catch to anything one does in life. The landlord said another couple was interested, and he had promised them the home. We established the fact that if the other person didn't come by noon, we got the house. He agreed.

We went over to have a quick lunch at Vick's tavern in Luckey, Ohio. The landlord had recommended Vick's restaurant, and he also recommended the fish sandwiches for lunch. We were on pins and needles because this was the house we wished to rent, and we had no other backup. We ate lunch with not too much interest in the food and went back to the house. By this time, he had over fifty calls; and later, we found that he had over two hundred calls for the house. He asked if we had any children. We said no. He said that we had the house. We made the arrangements to move in, and we were on cloud nine. We knew God had a hand in this rental as in all happenings in our lives!

Leaving Mansfield and Going to Rural Bowling Green

We had rented a U-Haul truck in Mansfield and had pulled it into our driveway at 21 Glenwood Boulevard. It took us a few hours on Friday night in early June to pack the truck, which tells you we didn't have a lot of possessions after a year and a half of marriage. However, we were proud of everything we owned, even though much of it was secondhand. We had everything on the truck on Friday night. This included our refrigerator, plugged into an extension cord. We kept the refrigerator running so all our refrigerated and frozen products would not spoil. Wasting food was not something in our vocabulary.

The truck was headed into the driveway, so it needed to be turned around so it could go out of the driveway facing the street. We tried backing out the truck, but it had a trailer hitch on it, which began to dig into the pavement. I tried to turn around the truck in the back of the property, but the hills on both sides wouldn't allow me to turn around. Our neighbor and good friend Benny said, "Let me try to turn the truck around." Benny revved up the engine, turned the wheel real sharp, and began to go forward up the hill. One tire of the front and one tire of the back were on the ground because of the two hills. In other words, it was teetering on two wheels, one back and one forth, with all our belongings in the truck. I thought the truck was going to tip over.

Just when we thought all was lost, Benny put the truck into reverse and gave it the juice. At this point, he had the truck half turned around. He turned the wheel toward the road and once again was three-fourths of the way turned around, teetering on a front wheel and a rear wheel. His last reverse placed the truck in a position 180 degrees from where it first started, and the truck was ready to go down the hill forward. As I got into the driver's seat and Kathy got into our car, we said our last goodbyes to a man who would do anything for us as he just proved in turning around the truck and almost hurting himself. Benny took a chance and allowed us to be able to go toward Bowling Green. If Benny hadn't turned around the truck, we could still be in Mansfield looking at our truck loaded with all our belongings. As I pulled out of the driveway, I noticed that the trailer hitch was very close to hitting the street.

Arriving at 21655 McCutchenville Road

As we pulled into our new home near Bowling Green with our dog, Missy, in tow, Walt, my oldest brother and his family were there to help us unload. Moving people in the Frederick family means you help others and others help you. After we were about done moving everything into the house, my landlord, Norm Brinker, came to the door with a quart of strawberries as a moving-in present. Norm came in and offered us the strawberries. He looked around at my niece and nephew and said, "Are these your children?" I assured him that they were Walt and Judy's kids, and I introduced him to everyone. As he displayed a big smile, the thought occurred to me that we had told him we didn't have any children, and here were several children.

Job Responsibilities in Lucas County

From 1969 until 1973, I was employed in the Lucas County Board of Mental Retardation and Developmental Disabilities. Working in a large county with over twenty departments to communicate and cooperate was no small feat. The majority of the workers were very cooperative, so the ability to offer quality programs was shared by many.

There were several areas in which I was responsible for the overall supervision and, in some cases, the direct provision of services as well. The major funding for the position came from a federal grant in recreation for adult consumers with mental retardation, most of them working in the workshop. The associated program for the school age was physical development. In Lucas County, the overall consumer base was 1,250 consumers. The provision of services in the physical therapy program was provided by a contract with physical therapists. The psychological services were provided first by a board employee and then by the Zucker Center under a contract for services. I later supervised these two departments and was responsible for the volunteer coordinator. A more specific look at the job responsibilities in each area will now be presented.

Recreation and Physical Education

There were three school locations for people in the school-age program, which was the ages of six to twenty-two. At each of these locations, I worked with the teachers and the students in physical development, otherwise known as physical education. The provision of training in the gross and fine motor skills were the major areas of concentration. The use of ballhandling skills, balance, running, and introduction to various games such as hockey, softball, and basketball at various skill levels were some of the areas of exposure.

Many of these skills were also involved in the Special Olympics program for children and adults in the state of Ohio. The Special Olympics program depends on volunteers, and the Toledo Jaycees provided the first funding and volunteers for this program in Lucas County. I had the privilege of being on the first Special Olympics governing board, the Ohio Athletic Association for the Mentally Retarded, in 1971. One of the programs involving basketball gave the students and adults the first chance to compete in this organized sport within Lucas County as well as other counties. In Special Olympics, participation is the important point.

The *Toledo Blade* did a special article on the basketball program on February 28, 1971, thanks to a contact within the Lucas County system. In this article, I am told, appeared one of the first pictures of a disabled person in the paper. The other challenge of this feature article was that

I told the *Toledo Blade* that I would do the story as long as the basketball coaches and cheerleader advisors were given credit for the program. The article came out on a Sunday.

The next day was a Monday. The coaches and cheerleader advisors felt they were not given enough credit and thought of leaving the program. They were right, and I told them the whole story. This incident did show me that people can understand even when they feel they have been wronged. This is the type of employee one wants on your side. This employee can work through the negatives that all of us experience at one time or another.

Additional public relations came about because of the basketball program for the Lucas County Board of Mental Retardation and Developmental Disabilities. Whenever the basketball games were played, I would call in the results of the game to local television stations such as WTOL TV-Channel 11 and WSPD-Channel 13 in Toledo.

One Friday evening after one of our teams, Larc Lane, played a basketball game, Kathy and I were invited over to the superintendent's house. Walt was a sports enthusiast, partially based on his talented wrestler son, Chris. As we listened to the sport results reporting all the area high school games, Larc Lane, Tracy and Heffner schools, and the Larc Lane workshop scores came on the air. It was a great feeling to see the whole county and area being exposed to the fact that people with disabilities were displaying their athletic abilities with their more normal peers. Several people had made this accomplishment possible. Walt had given endless hours to see the physical development program flourish by grant writing and administrative support. The coaches, players, parents, and I had come up with the everyday support to see that the basketball program flourished. The local television and newspapers also opened their news networks to reporting our scores and other activities.

The physical development program offered the opportunity to have the objectives of the physical development and recreation programs incorporated into the individual education program and the individual habilitation programs, which is the formal programs guide for students or adults in a structured program of instruction.

Special Olympics

It is appropriate that additional information on the Special Olympics program be provided at this time. The founder of the Special Olympics program was a remarkable person, Dick Ruff. Dick did not have the full use of his limbs. Both of his arms were missing—one above and one below his arm joint—and his leg was missing around the knee. Dick could golf, swim, and do about anything you and I could do. I was told that Dick was the placekicker for the Ohio State Buckeyes in his college years. Dick gave so much, and he died prematurely.

Another remarkable person and friend was Doug McVey from the Wood County Board of Mental Retardation. Together, we spearheaded the Northwest Ohio Special Olympics held at BGSU starting in 1971 and had a repeat performance another year. The program was run by students and other organizations such as the Toledo Jaycees and Fred Kossow and the United Commercial Travelers of America. The Northwest Regional Special Olympics allowed the participants to have a chance at competition for the State Special Olympics in track-and-field events. I can still remember sitting with Doug and other helpers the night before the first meet. As I sat there, I couldn't help but think, will this really go off as planned? Will the volunteers show? Will the officials show, and will the weather be nice? The trust I had in Doug and the rest of the people running the show paid off. Everyone did their part, and for the first such event, it looked like we had done it for years.

At times, we had special celebrities such as Dave Wottle, Olympic runner and gold medalist, and Sid Sink, nine-time All-American running star from BGSU, present and interacting with the participants. I never did figure out who had more fun, the participants or the celebrities. McDonald's restaurants served free over 1,300 hamburgers and orange drinks through owner Don Michel and manager Ed Ameen from their two restaurants. I didn't see how those two restaurants could serve their regular customers and jointly produce, transport, and serve all those hamburgers and drinks. Over the years, thousands and thousands of McDonald's hamburgers were to be served throughout the state of Ohio for Special Olympics. Cain's Potato Chips of Bowling Green donated chips for the lunch; and the United Commercial Travelers (UCT) insurance was present, serving its special charitable group, the mentally retarded. The UCT members manned a tent with games and prizes so that they were available for all participants. Fred not only coordinated UCT for the Special Olympics games, but he was also the head person of the scholarship fund for people involved with the developmentally disabled. Using small banks located at various stores, pennies, nickels, dimes, quarters, and half-dollars became dollars and hundreds of dollars so that teachers could be better educated and give better instruction to the developmentally disabled. Scholarships from the UCT were one of the sources of funds I used to obtain my advanced degrees. God knows money was tight.

One of the lessons I learned at a participant's expense was you cannot be safe enough in any of the events. When we had wheelchair races at the regional Special Olympics meet, one of the front wheels came off the ground. As the wheels went down, they turned sideways, and the wheelchair turned over with the participant hitting the track on the front of her body. There was no serious accident, but the event was not forgotten by anyone involved.

In the early 1970s, there were organized state training sessions for the Ohio Athletic Association's members. Dick procured room and board as well as a large hall for the presentations of physical development and recreation training. It was in the evening at a local pub that the members were introduced to a drink containing many different spirits. The drink was called the Killer. The drink almost lived up to its name.

It was at the beginning of the Special Olympics that I was asked to coordinate meals for the State Special Olympics Summer Games at Ohio State University. Kathy, sons Mark and Joe, and the Carpenters, Carol and Ron, as well as their children, Mark and Rhonda, were involved for over thirty years in the meals committee. Carol was for years the co-coordinator of this event. Several years ago, Michele Solether and her niece, Morgan, and nephew, Traver, became regulars. Michele developed systems that allowed over 20,000 meals to be served for athletes and coaches. Later, Michele and my son Mark became coordinators of the meals committee for the Summer Olympics. I must mention Ron and Mary Jo Bosch as they have worked to provide family volunteers to assemble and serve 8,000 meals each summer. Many challenges such as frozen orange juice, rain, loss of food sponsors, and other conditions were dealt with as they occurred. I marvel at volunteers who keep coming back year after year to work in the hot sun to provide the necessary meals.

One of the most moving parts of the Ohio State Special Olympics is when the law enforcement agencies come together for the Olympic torchlight at Jesse Owens Memorial Stadium. This included the Ohio State Highway Patrol, sheriff departments, and local police agencies from throughout the state. There were initially around twenty police motorcycles all with their lights on, fifty runners, and fifty bicycle riders who have brought the Olympic torch from all corners of the state. As the last torch runner is on the field, the helicopter representing the Columbus Police Department hovers over the stadium. The Special Olympics torch is lit, and one knows for sure at that point that one is part of an incredible happening where everyone involved is honored to be present.

Toledo Jaycees

I had been indoctrinated at a very young age that not only did one owe it to give back to their community but also giving back from a professional status was good not only for me but also for the organization. No person or organization of a for profit or not for profit can exist in a vacuum, for sooner or later, it will die for lack of business or lack of tax or donation monies. That is why the Toledo Jaycees is spotlighted here. For it to be successful, it is necessary for people to learn from organizations and to give their time and energy and for each party to be able to profit from each other.

I had been involved with the Jaycees as it had been involved with the Special Olympics program in Lucas County. If the Jaycees had not been involved with the Special Olympics in Lucas County, there may not have been a Special Olympics there for several years.

After the Special Olympics in 1971, I was asked by the Toledo Jaycees to be a member. Involvement with organizations, especially organizations that worked closely with the Lucas County Board, was seen as desirable and necessary to the success of the program for people with mental retardation and developmental disabilities. Involvement with organizations would be a theme throughout my employment as these contacts allowed me to open many doors for the population I was to serve. For this reason, among others, I joined and in 1972 was appointed a director in the Toledo Jaycees. In this capacity, I had projects I had the responsibility of seeing through. This fact also gave me management experience with people from several different backgrounds.

More on Special Olympics

As was previously mentioned, Special Olympics was becoming big in Ohio. In Lucas County, one of the best basketball players was Delbert Brent. Delbert was a handsome teenage Afro-American student at Tracy School. As a star basketball player, he was to go to the state tournament with his team. Unfortunately, a team from Bellefontaine, Ohio, was better; and they won the state tournament that year. During the school year, *The Toledo Blade* did attend one of Tracy School's regular games, and Delbert was featured on the sports page. It was a new area for the handicapped and people with mental retardation and developmental disabilities.

In addition to the basketball team, we had cheerleaders. Bertha Steele was a teacher and coordinated the cheerleaders. Over time, the girls became very good at leading the cheers.

International Special Olympics

My last year at Lucas County saw me going with two students from the school to the International Special Olympics in Chicago, Illinois, at Soldier Field. From the time we arrived in Chicago until the day we left, we were treated like royalty. When we arrived, we were ushered into this large hall in which many games and other activities were taking place. The two students had a great time.

During the competition, Jeannie, an attractive teenage girl, was in the 100-yard dash. She took either a gold or a silver medal. She was overjoyed as was I. Another male student, Jimmy, also successfully competed at these games.

Recreation

As I began to work with other members of the staff, there was a major stumbling block, and that was the fact that no dancing was permitted at board functions. Time and time again, it came to me that there was to be no dancing. The only way we thought we had a chance of changing that policy was coming up with a questionnaire that showed the board the desire for this activity to be reinstated. This questionnaire involved consumer participation in all types of recreation programs. Within this questionnaire, there was a question if parents thought dancing should be allowed at board functions, and if not, why not. There were hundreds of responses that came back from the 1,250 families who had a son or daughter in the program. After all the results were tallied, there was one person who objected to dancing, and that was from a religious viewpoint.

We went through superintendent Walt Solarz to ask the board if we could have dancing since there was little objection to this normal activity. We walked into the board meeting with all our findings. Remember that a board meeting is usually a very threatening event for presenters as any question that is asked must have not only an answer but also a good answer. The time came for the presentation on the recreation questionnaire report. We went through many of the findings showing that our population was listening to the radio and watching television many more hours a day than they were exercising. When I said, "I would like to talk a little about dancing because I understand the board does not allow dancing at board functions," I no more than got the words "board functions" out of my mouth when several board members said, "We never said you can't have dancing." So, I said, "That means we can hold dances." All the board members said yes. I learned a valuable lesson; you never really know the answer unless you ask!

I was speechless. I asked no more questions but took their answer, and did we ever have dances. If there would have been available a computer program with a statistical multiple regression analysis, Dr. Robert Blackwell and I would have published one of the finest studies ever done on the analysis of recreation programs and the mentally retarded.

Work availability in a sheltered workshop has its ups and downs. When work is available, workers are happy and busy. When work is slack, there is little to do. This point of activity is why the federal grant was written, to offer worthwhile activities for workshop employees during slack times. The solution offered was to have various leisure time activities available that would provide not only activities but also constructive activities. This would mean that people in the workshop were able to enjoy activities and profit skill-wise from their involvement. To aid in the instructional portion of the project, the steps to learn the activity were analyzed in a developmental scheme using the developmental task form. With this form, the usefulness and ease in learning would be enhanced.

An example of one of the common activities is playing cards. Its useful skills learned could be eye-hand coordination, finger dexterity, shape and color recognition, and number similarity and differences. Let us look at the first step in learning cards that would be manipulating and dealing cards. In dealing, finger dexterity is learned. The learner would then separate cards according to color using a regular deck. Cards would then be separated by suits and then number or face cards. We are now learning shape, number, and color recognition. A matching game using a few numbers can be learned, and then adding more cards until a person is able to match several cards would be taught. Other card games from simple to complex would be taught. Over fifty various games and activities were analyzed so that examples from less active activities, such as cards, to very active activities, such as basketball, were presented. This information was compiled and published by Mafex Associates, Inc. Publishers in Johnstown, Pennsylvania. The title of the book was *Manual for Constructive Leisure Time Activities*. Dr. Blackwell and I were the coauthors.

One interesting thing behind the scenes is that much of my writing was done while I was squirrel hunting. I have always enjoyed multitasking, and this was no exception. I was a pretty good shot with seven shots producing seven squirrels. The bonus was that I had seven meals from the seven squirrels.

Professional Writings

When I entered my first position in Richland County, I made it a goal to have one professional paper published in a national journal for physical development each year. From 1967 until 1973, I had six articles published. As I reviewed my writings, I found that I had published five articles and coauthored a book in the area of physical development. Much of the credit for my publications goes to Steve Woitovich, superintendent of Richland County, and Dr. Julian Stein with the American Association for Health, Physical Education, and Recreation in Washington, D.C. Dr. Stein was the editor of *Challenge* and always encouraged my publications.

Other Related Happenings in the Lucas County System

A Dance

We have looked at the reintroduction of dancing in the Lucas County system. After the dances had started up, there was one dance that I will never forget. It was a dance in the multipurpose room at the Larc Lane adult workshop. The dance was underway, and the music was very loud. But it was the way the dancers liked to be happy and have fun. Everyone was having fun. One of the very large adults, let us call him Jim, was very upset about something and was not having fun. I noticed Jim's behavior and was making my way over to him when I saw a chair flying across the floor. I looked back to the source of the chair, and there was Jim in a very negative mood.

I was concerned about Jim, but I was also concerned about the other dancers. I knew he had his times, but I was in charge, and I needed to get him out of the room. I walked up to him, who was a good foot taller than me, and I said, "Jim, I want to meet you outside right now." I didn't know if he would listen, and I didn't know what he was going to do, but I started to walk out. By this time, the music had stopped, and the crowd of people in the room were watching us. As I started to walk out, I looked out of the corner of my eye and saw Jim coming. I thought that this was good, he would be out of the room, but what was I going to do once I got outside?

We walked outside. I looked at Jim, and he looked at me. Somehow, the thought came to me, *Tell Jim you do not want to fight, and ask if he wants to fight.* I said, "Jim, I don't want to fight. Do you want to fight?" He looked me square in the eye and said, "No." Thankfully, things had de-escalated, and we had a very constructive talk. I bet that if I saw Jim on the street, he would still treat me as nice as he did after our little talk. Sometimes, it happens that there is no explanation for the outcome, but there is a chance of something positive if other people trust one another to be understanding.

Torch

In 1972, the Toledo City Department of Recreation called several people together who either had a disability or worked in the area of the handicapped. The staff came up with the acronym TORCH, which stood for Toledo's Organized Recreation for the Community's Handicapped. There were several distinguished community members on the board. Chuck Buckenmyer was the Director of Recreation for the City of Toledo; Jack Steward was head of the transportation system for the city; Art Edgerton was, among other things, host of a TV show; and Ed Schmakel was director of alumni relations at the University of Toledo. I was chosen to be the president of the board. With the guidance of the board and the energy of the recreation staff, the program received notoriety for its several positive programs. This was one of the first such programs of its kind nationally. I also enjoyed serving on this innovative board and program.

In 1976, the *Toledo Blade* printed a feature article on the TORCH program. The program was informative and positive on a summer day program funded by Champion Spark Plug of Toledo. In a letter to the editor, I recognized the *Toledo Blade*'s positive contribution to society made in this article. It was nice to see something other than articles on incidents of crime, violence, and disagreements.

More about the Students and Workshop Employee

Matt Kruse

A student at Larc Lane and Special Olympian was Matt. Matt was a person with Down syndrome and always had a smile and friendly manner about him. I was to know his mother, Kitty, as she was extremely active in programs through the Catholic church for persons with developmental disabilities. I can remember meeting with her and Fr. Hiltz at the Hillcrest Hotel in Toledo to organize various programs in the church for persons with special needs.

While doing research on Matt, I found he passed in December of 2012 at the age of fifty-two. Matt continued to be involved in many church-related organizations and was an usher at Little Flower Parish in the Toledo area. Matt was one of many persons I had contact with who went on to do many noteworthy activities.

Delbert Brent

Delbert, as mentioned several prior times, was a very high-functioning male who was exceptionally talented in sports. He was a member of the school-age basketball team. He led his team to the state tournament in Special Olympics at BGSU. I am told that in a special article on the basketball program in Lucas County, he was one of the first persons with mental retardation to have his picture in the local paper, the *Toledo Blade*. Delbert, like many other boys and girls in the program, were to have their self-image enhanced with their success in sports, usually through the Special Olympics program.

Two Brothers

Bill and Bob were in their late twenties or early thirties. They were Jewish and had both been born with mental retardation and developmental disabilities. Bill was older and was of stocky build. Bob was younger and thin. They were both good in athletics and dearly loved to play basketball. I remember whenever Bill was put into the basketball game, he would always clap his hands together, happy to be put into the game.

Their father owned a business and was friends with many very influential people. Their mother was attractive and active in the parents' association. The father was involved with many other parents and was the president of an association to build a residential center in Toledo. In one of my future jobs, I was responsible for state funding of residential centers and had many meetings with this parent and others to raise money for this center. I remember going to lunch with him at an exclusive steak house named Johnny's. When we ate, he would order drinks and steak for both of us and would never pay the bill. He must have had an expense account and charged it. At the time, it was impressive.

Chuck

One of the other adults was a young man in his early twenties. Chuck was a person with Down syndrome. He had red hair and carried messages and letters from the workshop to the school to be mailed. Chuck was a basketball player and was overjoyed whenever he would make a basket.

Other Special People

Tommy Stang

When I began dating Kathy, I was introduced to one of her cousins, Tommy. Tommy was at that time a young person with profound mental retardation and also cerebral palsy. Tommy, like so many others, had a mother and father who would do anything for their special son. Tommy was one of five sons and fit well into the family. Due to Tommy's special needs, the bathroom in their house was converted by his father, Norb, so that Grace could bath Tommy, as he had grown so that it was impossible to wash him in a regular bathtub. Tommy had to have all of his food blended so that he could consume it. He was taken to many of their social gatherings and was thus a part of the community. I can remember Tommy being there when we went ice skating, camping or other social events.

Tommy lived into his teens, and it was a sad day when he left this world. I was always amazed at how well his parents and siblings made Tommy a part of their family life and the community.

Jerry Trabbic

Jerry Trabbic was our friend. He may also have been a relative or neighbor who attended our church, but we were friends. Some of us were old friends; some of us were new friends. With Jerry, he knew us all as a friend. Old friends had little preference over new friends. Jerry had a gift; he would walk into a room and start shaking hands with new friends and old friends. He would talk with you whether he knew you for one minute or years. Jerry could, as the saying goes, work a room as good as any politician. I have watched Jerry's brothers and his father, Cliff, walk into a room and either renew friendships or make new friends. Jerry had some excellent role models in this respect. Jerry would have given Will Rogers a run for his money because Jerry, like Will, could say, "I never met a man I didn't like."

Another point that needs to be made is Jerry cared deeply about people. He would listen to you, and he would respect your point of view. He was not a judge but a cooperator.

Jerry had enrolled in Wood Lane Industries and was working and making great progress. Jerry was off a short time from the workshop because of an illness. He wanted to go over to see all his fellow workers at the workshop; so, Don, his older brother, took him over. After his visit, I asked Don how his visit went after being absent for a period. Don said Jerry walked into the shop and said something like "I am coming back" as he raised his hands in the air. I hear he received a very warm verbal reception from his fellow workers. One could see that Jerry loved his fellow workers. One could also see that Jerry had endeared his fellow workers to him, and they showed this support.

In the middle of March of 2008, I first heard that Jerry's health was deteriorating. We gave Jerry his celebration of life on June 26, 2008.

I am proud to say that I knew Jerry. I am even prouder to say that Jerry was my friend, and I really loved him, and I miss him. I am sure that everyone who knew Jerry would say these words.

Chuck Heermeier

When we moved into our new home on N. River Road near Pemberville, Ohio, we discovered that there was a young man, Chuck, who would walk in front of our home on occasion. Chuck lived a short distance from our house with his parents and from birth had a deformed face; his parents had constantly searched for a surgeon who could repair his face, without any success. Chuck knew our boys and was always friendly with our family.

In later years, Chuck went to a facility for the handicapped in a neighboring county and was to die there years later. We will always remember Chuck as a person who tried to adapt to a world that didn't truly understand his daily trials.

CHAPTER 3

The Early Years of Our Sons, Joe and Mark

Joe Is First

The Grand Announcement

In an office communication dated May 8, 1972, to the staff of the Lucas County Board of Mental Retardation and Developmental Disabilities titled "All Interested Parties" from Joe and Kathy Frederick, the following message was distributed: "In an attempt to dispel any rumors, it is our pleasure to announce that a bundle of joy will be arriving in the Frederick household sometime in December. The baby will be our first in over four and a half years of marriage. For further information, you may contact either Kathy or Joe on Cloud 9." The message was received with many smiles and congratulations.

Presentation at the Superintendent Conference

The day after the birth of Joe, November 17, 1972, I was scheduled to make a presentation to the Superintendent's Association of the County

Boards of Mental Retardation and Developmental Disabilities in Columbus on my programs involving physical development. I asked Kathy if she would mind if I went. Although she wanted to see me the day after the birth of Joe, she knew it was important for me to give the presentation. I told her that I would arrange for someone to take my place and visit her since I would be in Columbus. My right-hand man at the time was John Pristash. John had worked for me for a few years; I trusted him to visit Kathy. The presentation went well, and John visited Kathy in Toledo. When I came back from Columbus, I immediately went to see Kathy. From that point on, we began to realize a little bit more every day that the addition to the Frederick family was to produce more changes in all phases of our lives than we had ever begun to imagine.

Mark Was Next

Elvis Presley

It was New Year's Eve 1976, and we were invited by our friends Carol and Ron Carpenter and a few of Carol's relatives to attend a concert by "the King" Elvis Presley with fifty thousand fans. After the opening acts, we were all ready to see a great performance. As Elvis was to come on stage, the entire Silverdome Stadium in Pontiac, Michigan, went dark. The introductory music came on loud, and the spotlight focused on the main stage. It was so exciting that all I could see on the other side of the stage was thousands of camera bulbs go off. As Elvis came to our side of the stage, I began taking pictures. I didn't want to miss a shot. It was then I noticed that I had my lens cap on my camera. I did miss a few shots. Then an unexpected event happened—Elvis had split his pants. By accident, I caught the split on my camera.

The evening was one of the most entertaining we have ever experienced. Elvis was truly "the King." The performance was great, and the encore nine months later was a very personal experience as Mark was to come into our lives. This was because Kathy and I had attended the Elvis Presley concert, and as a result of attending the performance, it was projected that "We Were All Shook Up."

Mark Is Born

The birth of our second son, Mark, was a bit easier than our first son, Joe. The reason was simple; we had been through it once. There is no joy greater than observing life. This time around, I was in the delivery room and experienced firsthand seeing the entire birth. We did not know if we were going to have a boy or a girl. As this baby was coming into the world, I gained an immense amount of respect for Kathy. The obstetrician said, "The shoulders are too big to be a girl." He was right; we had a boy. It was September 18, 1976, when Mark decided that he was to come into this world at St. Vincent Hospital in Toledo, Ohio.

PART II

Moving My Workplace from the County to the State Government

CHAPTER 4

Educational Consultant Serving Nineteen Counties in Northwest Ohio

General Duties

While I had enjoyed my past two jobs as physical education and recreation director in Richland and Lucas counties, my educational credentials and desire to work with many counties led me to a position with the state of Ohio. In 1973, I accepted the position as program consultant with the nineteen counties in Northwest Ohio. The position was very encompassing and included several areas I had experience. I was to remain in this position until 1976. I was to accept a new position as district manager in 1975 but was to keep the program consultant position until funds were available for a replacement in 1976.

In this position, I was responsible for approving programs and their state funding for nineteen county boards of mental retardation and developmental disabilities. I did not have direct supervision over employees in these county programs, so it was back to some of my previous experiences of indirectly supervising people. I had found that in indirect supervision, tactfully working with people was a necessary component in being successful. Indirect supervision involves being responsible to see that program objectives are achieved by other people, but the ability to hire and fire is not present. I found that programs and services were usually in good shape, and therefore, supervision of people was made easier.

The position of educational consultant was an interesting role. While I was responsible to oversee that the programs conformed to the rules of the state of Ohio Division of Mental Retardation for County Boards of Mental Retardation and Developmental Disabilities, when change was needed, the role of consultant was a bit more challenging. When everything is going well in the county programs, being a consultant is a doable position. When change is needed, I saw my role as a helper with the county rather than a dictator. As a state inspector, being able to provide guidance so that solutions were implemented was essential. The end goal for both sides was that program services and ultimately the people being served by the program would benefit. I learned real early in working with other people that a positive approach will help more than a more negative one. Fortunately, the county board personnel were cooperative people.

Role of the Board and Superintendent

This section was one of the most difficult sections of the entire book to write. One reason it is so difficult to write is that no two boards or superintendents/administrators are alike. The next reason it is difficult to write is that knowing how people think in each of these roles is many times difficult to predict.

There are certain givens that will help us understand this relationship. In working with any county board, it was important that the board and superintendent had roles, knew them, and implemented them fairly. Fairly should mean that any decisions made were for the benefit of the clients being served. The roles of the board and administrator seem similar in private and public boards and organizations. The role of the board as the policymaker and the superintendent as administrator is simply put the essential part of these two positions. It is very clear in the laws for the county board of developmental disabilities that there was a separation of duties between the board and the superintendent. It was also possible that the board members and the superintendent did not follow the letter of the law and allow their positions to overlap. For example, the board members' position was to make policies; and while they shouldn't, they may at times also administer staff that the superintendent should be administering. Keeping these two job duties separate is important because the board member or chairperson should not do the job of the superintendent, nor should the superintendent do the board's duties. If the board was making the policies and administering the program, there would be two direct line bosses, the administrator or the superintendent being one and a board member being the second. In this case, where the board member periodically becomes the administrator, to whom does the staff listen and take direction? Is it the administrator or the board member? Any situation like this, places everyone in the organization in confusion. Any organization with a board and an administrator must be careful to do its job and only its job.

Practices in which the superintendent and board do not carry out their respective jobs efficiently will make it impossible to have a good working relationship between the two. Usually, open communications can help solve these misunderstandings. Having administrative rules that the board and staff follow is another must. Rules provide consistency for all employees, the board members, and anyone associated with the organization.

While many boards and superintendents have developed positive relationships, the opposite is also true in that boards may get into administrative duties, not have the entire story, and take actions on this limited information. I decided very early in this management game that if the employment I was in with my board or my employer was developing into an unworkable conclusion, I would look for another job. A bad relationship, for whatever reason, between the administrator and the board or other employer would usually be hard to work out, especially if there was no resolution in sight, and the board or administrator or both were not willing to work out the situation. In this situation, ultimately, the harm to the organization and more importantly the people to be served will usually only grow. My experience with many boards or employers is they are willing to work toward a fair solution. Unfortunately, others are not, and a no-win situation is a common result. Leaving the situation may be the best result yet not the desired result for some of the involved administrators.

An Interesting Parent

While in this position, I was to meet many interesting people. In Hancock County, south of Wood County, I was walking through the workshop and noticed some workers. This was the time when recycling was getting popular, and they were recycling metal in the form of beverage cans. The aluminum cans were separated from the steel cans by passing them under a magnet.

One of the workers in the workshop had a most interesting father. His name was Fred Graff. He was a retired Army officer. I got to know Fred as he was now a teacher in physical education at Findlay College and very active in the local Special Olympics program. His son was in the program. I was to work with Fred on many Special Olympics programs.

Another parent from one of the northwestern counties was Terry. He had a young son in one of the programs and was to work very hard to start a residential center. Unfortunately, one of his children was to be tragically killed in a traffic accident.

Working with the Ohio Division of Mental Retardation and Developmental Disabilities

Mental Retardation and Mental Illness

I would like to address a common misunderstanding between the terms "mental illness" and "mental retardation." They are not the same, although it is possible for a person to possess both conditions at one time.

In a 1975 newspaper article, I came across an article that confused these two conditions. I informed the paper, the *Toledo Blade*, that I wished to clear up these two definitions; and it was printed in the editorial page.

My understanding of mental retardation is that it is a condition in which the person's intelligence does not allow them to attain their full potential in terms of learning and applying it. Mental illness is a term for a person who usually has normal intellectual abilities but has severe emotional disturbances.

Time to Move On

An opening as the district IV manager with the Division of Mental Retardation and Developmental Disabilities, the Department of Mental Health and Mental Retardation, for the ten counties in Northwest Ohio came open. It was a management position and involved a great deal of responsibility. I talked with several professional friends and, of course, my wife about the position. The position seemed right, the staff was competent, and I needed to return to management. So, another chapter of my life is unfolding.

CHAPTER 5

District Manager and Other Positions

Background

In early 1975, I was appointed to the position of district manager. My prior positions had prepared me for this latest appointment. For example, in 1967, I had started my career in mental retardation and developmental disabilities in Mansfield as the physical education and recreation director. After two years in Mansfield, we left for employment in Toledo in the Lucas County Board of Mental Retardation and Developmental Disabilities in a similar-type position that I had just left. Going to Toledo allowed both me and Kathy to further our education. Another four years passed, and in 1973, I had a chance for advancement with the State Department of Mental Retardation and Developmental Disabilities (MRDD) as an educational consultant. In this state position, I was responsible for the development, coordination, funding, monitoring, licensing, and evaluation of community services and programs for the ten counties in Northwestern Ohio. After completing my master's degree from BGSU in 1970, I felt I was ready for this challenge. Some people have chidingly told me at this point in my career that four jobs in six years exemplified well the principle that I could not hold a job.

The many happenings that will be covered in this chapter as in other chapters were firsthand information that I knew well because they were part of my job. The happenings of central office and state, the district office, and the county boards of MRDD was information that, daily, I needed to know and use. Much of the information I was personally involved with providing. The television and newspaper articles often quoted me or others in my office. In dealing with the public relations network, we needed to be honest about the information we made public. If information was privileged, we needed to protect the clients, the communities, the department, and our job. Sometimes, it was a tough call; but wherever possible, information was conveyed to the public. We were, in fact, dealing with people's rights or the civil rights of people with mental retardation and developmental disabilities. The issues to be solved were existing, challenging, and required in many cases an attitudinal or monetary change in the provision of services.

District Office
Five Jobs in One
District Manager

Taking over the reins of the district office had its uneasy times. This would be the first time I was responsible as CEO for a large office at twenty-nine years of age. The staff was to grow from eleven to twenty-five people because of federal grants such as CETA and Vista. Major services provided were overseeing and providing public relations and planning with the nine counties in Northwest Ohio. Providing case management services for people in need and instituting a client flow system through a central data bank and process of placement and follow-up required twenty-four-hours-a-day, seven-days-a-week services by the staff. Bottom line was that many services such as lodging and food were essential for all clients, and many did not adequately possess these resources. Working to expand services for the community, including the county boards of mental retardation and development disabilities, was challenging in that some counties had funds to expend on these social services and some did not. Administering the purchase of service funds for residential services as well as development of residential homes were important aspects of the provision of services. The program consultant was responsible for monitoring and evaluating programs with the county boards of mental retardation and developmental disabilities through early intervention, school-age, and adult programs. Licensure of residential facilities was a yearly review and quarterly monitoring. Organizing and providing services in needed areas was constant with the ever-changing directions of the programs. A closer look at these services is important to understand the breadth of services to people with mental retardation and developmental disabilities. It is only through close monitoring, consultation, and coordination can the changes with the community and state agencies take place.

Capital Construction

As the district manager and residential consultant, I looked at the capital construction of residential homes from two different viewpoints. As district manager, I looked at all the construction in the entire district; and as residential consultant, I looked at all the projects and all the specifics of the homes. Residential development was at this time exploding as many counties were looking at returning their county residents who had lived in the state institutions back to their home county. Group homes were somewhat common in counties, and many residents were housed in the state institutions run by the state of Ohio. In the ten counties in Northwest Ohio between 1975 and 1979, there were ten residential homes in the process of building or remodeling at a total cost of $4,233,281. This meant that 169 people would have or continue to have their residences. Seeing residents come home to their county of origin or remain in their county of residence and be close to their families and the resources of their county provided positive living circumstances for those involved.

Support services such as maintenance, transportation, and other auxiliary services were needed for all the programs administered by the county board of mental retardation and developmental disabilities. There were five such support service buildings at $129,344.

Overview of Duties

The various tasks of the district office required people with expertise in each of their areas. As in every management position, the easy solutions to challenges do not always come easy. The ability to work with other people and organizations requires that from the top managers down, everyone must work together. Boards of organizations work with their executive directors who worked with me, and my people required all of us to be on the same song sheet. Sometimes, these song sheets require written agreements; other times, they are verbal. The risks that are to be taken in all phases of program provision must be carefully assessed so the clients are the winners. There were several community leaders whose expertise and contacts were essential to success. Specials requests by families for services needed by clients who were either alive or had passed we tried to respect. I was to find early in administration that being nice to everyone was essential. It is essential because it is the right thing to do, and tomorrow, they or you may be gone.

Residential Developer

As was just pointed out, residential development was another major component of the district office. Since residential development was an extremely important development at this time and funding was an issue, as was the attitude of the neighborhood, I had the privilege of taking on the responsibilities as the residential developer for one year because of the lack of funds. This position entailed knowing the residential needs in each county, working with the counties to find grants for the twenty new residential facilities in process, and working with the counties to obtain operational funds and the acceptance of people with mental retardation and developmental disabilities in their neighborhood. Monitoring existing homes in terms of the provision of appropriate services was very time consuming, challenging, and entailed working with communities, advocate groups, and others who had an interest in existing residential homes. Although it was unusual, a few homes were asked to close their doors because of inadequate care. Another major variable to be addressed was zoning for proposed homes. In these times, neighborhoods needed more understanding of people with disabilities. Our next section will review some trying public meetings in which the rights of the developmentally disabled were addressed.

Program Consultant

I came into this position with two jobs, the educational consultant for District Three out of Lima and District Four out of Toledo. Since a hiring freeze was statewide, I needed to carry on both these educational consulting positions with my other three new positions associated with the district manager job. We will not duplicate information about the duties of the educational consulting position just described in the previous chapter.

NODC Construction

The fifth major job responsibility and position was to oversee the planning, coordination, and development of the program and twelve buildings for the $8.5 million Northwest Ohio Developmental Center (NODC). These buildings would house 177 residents admitted by the district office into NODC. The plans on the development and refinement of policies and procedures affecting the admissions, discharge, respite care, and other services for NODC was the responsibility of my office. I was the acting superintendent until August 1976 when Ray Anderson was chosen as superintendent by the selection committee.

More on the Programs at NODC

The developmental center was to provide transitional programming for people who will usually remain for a few months up to three years. The programming they will receive will be on an individual basis on an everyday, twenty-four-hour-a-day basis. The environment will be humane. The short-term residential treatment will serve as a transition point for people moving through state mental retardation facilities to community settings.

The Energy to Do All These Jobs

With this background, we can now look at more specifics in my work and my private life. Little did I know upon entering these positions that my energy level would need to grow more than I could possibly imagine. I would need every bit of energy that I naturally possessed, and I was not sure where the additional energy source originated. I had beliefs in God and is ability to give and mine to receive this positive energy and consequently positive deeds or actions. My belief that my twin, who had died in utero before my birth, was a part of my life and mysteriously I would receive energy from my twin for this task seemed real to me. Other people in my life and internal energy were sources of energy that I believe are present., and I can identify from others giving me positive interactions and knowledge, and I am able to at times link them to help me spring into action. These forms of energy or help should continue to be observable in my writings.

The downside of energy can be perception by others. Fast motions and quick problem-solving can be uncomfortable for others. I did not hide my enthusiasm, which was often exemplified in my fast actions, until I sensed my actions were making me ineffective with others. In one program evaluation, I was coined "Like a dog chasing a car." When I read this, I knew that I needed to look closer at my actions.

Issues in the District Office

Deinstitutionalization

A major emphasis of the district office was to see that the objectives of deinstitutionalization were adopted. Many of the people with mental retardation and developmental disabilities were living in state facilities called institutions or at home with their parents, and a few were living in community homes. The focus of the MRDD was to move people from the state facilities and into group homes or other appropriate homes in the community. The community is where every person has the right to live. At this time, few homes existed, and the funding for these homes was just developing. The development of group homes and procurement of the funding were the responsibilities of the district office. Institutions could have over one thousand residents, and group homes could typically have four to eight residents. Living in the community allowed residents to use the community resources, such as grocery stores, clothing stores, restaurants, recreation areas, and other resources, which didn't always exist in the large institutions.

The Partnership of Local Groups, the County Boards of Mental Retardation and Developmental Disabilities, and the District Office

No partnership was perfect, yet the development of some type of system was essential between the district office and county boards of MRDD. The district office with its planning, coordination, development, and placement of residents into residential facilities and other services needed capital and operating funds. County board service was at the apex in the development of a successful system. There were many challenges in working through this process. The success rested on the partnership between the state, the county and the other local providers.

Within each county were several service delivery systems in which organizations and even families were the providers of residential services. In a report by Jeanne Lippert from the District Four office in December 1978, there were twelve residential homes in process for 248 people, and several letters of intent had been submitted for hundreds of community residential beds from state residential funding.

The results from these partnerships produced many success stories that allowed people from institutions/developmental centers and the community to live in or remain in a typical neighborhood. The acceptance by other neighbors has in most cases been very positive. The ability to hold jobs, shop at the local stores, sleep in their own room, have family meals, and, yes, even take vacations is the result of many working toward a common goal—normal living.

Case Management

Case management is the central social worker who oversees the planning of services for people with mental retardation and developmental disabilities and works with the family and other community agencies. Many times, the beginning of service is to assess the needs of the individual and then plan and provide information and referral on services. An underlying principle is to protect the rights of the person being served.

It is essential to develop and use a plan so that services can be identified, coordinated, accessed, monitored, and provided. The provision of direct services out of the district office is often given by other agencies, not the district office. The provision of services may be in several areas such as a comprehensive evaluation, residential, health/medical, professional services, behavioral, counseling, and the legal area of guardianship, trusteeship, and protectorship. Emergency or crisis services and respite care are often services needed now. The accessing of state and federal funds is essential to accessing services. The case management services or social worker services while not a contract service in the district office would be soon.

Being a big part of the overall management of a person's life in terms of their daily needs and services could be a challenge. The direction of the plan required research and available resources. Being a case manager was a pleasure in a position of serving the rights of this population.

There were many cases in which the use of case management did not seem to be present. One case that many would say case management planning was questionable was in the rights of a baby in Washington, D.C. National attention was given several years ago to the case of a Down syndrome or mongoloid baby at the Johns Hopkins University Hospital in Baltimore, Maryland. The baby had an intestinal blockage that prohibited digestion. For fifteen days, the parents did not allow the doctors to operate. The baby starved to death. This was not the only case like this I was familiar with. There are many cases where human beings die because of their life condition, and case management may not be a part of this process.

Another unforgettable case that helps us understand the variables of case management was out of my office. There was a man who had lived forty-seven years in an institution. Recent legislation gave residents certain rights to leave institutions. Therefore, in 1978, he was living in the Toledo area. He had stolen a cab in Chicago and had lived in several group homes and under viaducts near highways. The weather was getting cold, so outside living was becoming dangerous. Twice in a short period, I was called to pick up this resident. The police in Woodville, Ohio, called me as the district manager and head of the office very early on a weekday morning to locate assistance in transporting this person to his dwelling. I decided to go to Woodville and transport the person to his group home.

When I picked up Ralph, the officer told me he had hitched a ride on the turnpike and had emptied the mailboxes from where he exited the turnpike to Woodville. The mail was returned, and I transported the person to his boarding home. A few days later, I received a call from the Libbey Glass Company in Rossford, Ohio, telling me this same person had no place to live and needed a ride to his home. I again decided to pick up this person early in the morning. He was returned to his home. I received an experience that helped me better understand the role of my case managers. While this person had lived in many group homes and other residences, he would decide that day to leave his present dwelling, which he was legally able to do. Although we made available different placements and programs, he didn't like them. He left the city because he didn't agree with the options available to him.

Other Issues on Rights of the Mentally Retarded

One very successful progressive city zoning ordinance was passed through the city of Toledo, with the cooperation of the Old West End Association and the District Four office. It was the first such zoning ordinance for the mentally retarded in Ohio. This zoning allowed group homes to be established so that they could exist in a fair manner for all people involved.

In a case that came through the district office in September 1976 via the *Toledo Blade*, a lady was planning to move to Honolulu with her two mentally retarded sons. She was told that she and her sons couldn't stay in that state. We informed her via the paper and personally of the family's right to move and stay. Luckily, I had the resources of attorneys through my employer to check legalities.

Another rights issue for people with mental retardation and developmental disabilities was to vote. Laws did not exist at this time that restricted a person's ability to vote because of being mentally retarded and developmentally disabled.

A related issue in deinstitutionalization was the issue of community placement being better than the institutional setting. Individual examples have gone both ways on this issue, and a person being in the least restrictive setting is an important consideration. The placement needs to be right for the resident.

The placement of residents is a paramount issue. If a resident is to be released from an institution and the institution is in county A but the county of residence is from county B, why should county A pay for a resident who came from another county such as county B? One argument used is that the state takes money from the institution as it is no longer spending money on this person who is leaving the institution. Therefore, county A isn't spending its money on another county's resident. The other argument is that the county of residence is the first place for a person to try their community placement.

Edward S. and Edward B.

In March 1975, I had been in the office early when one of my employees informed me that Edward S.'s mother had visited the group home and claimed that the person she was told was her son was not her son. She was to claim in a lawsuit that her son died on October 22, 1972, and the nursing home had concealed this fact from her. She first learned of the death of her son on April 1973 when she visited the home. A lawsuit was filed by the mother of Edward S. in March 1975.

The other involved resident was Edward B. When interviewed about the burial, Edward B.'s father was certain that he had buried his own son. Both the Edwards were placed in the same nursing home in Toledo from Apple Creek Center located near Apple Creek, Ohio. While the paperwork confirmed that the dead child was Edward B. and that Edwards S. was alive in the nursing home, my office conducted a coordinated investigation with Apple Creek and the central office to investigate the questions on the identity of these two residents.

All the available paperwork was examined, and the direct care worker from Apple Creek familiar with the case traveled to Toledo to view the remaining resident. The results of the investigation were handed over to the court, which settled the case with the involved people. I never knew the actual settlement because the case was between the involved parties. I also was instructed not to release any of the information from the investigation as it was conducted to settle a private lawsuit.

Several years later, I was at the state convention for the Ohio Association of County Boards of Mental Retardation and Developmental Disabilities (OACBMRDD) when my contact person from Apple Creek, a man named Paul, in charge of its investigation in this case approached me. He asked me if I had heard the latest on the Edward S. and Edward B. lawsuit. I said that I had not heard anything, and I had not talked to anyone about the case other than people such as himself who had been involved in the investigation. He told me that it was all over the news in Cleveland as the case had been made public, and the person buried on October 22, 1972, was Edward S., not Edward B. The family of Edward S. was going to exhume the body and place it in the proper burial plot. Shortly after that, a member from Edward S.'s family contacted me and invited me to the exhuming of the body and the reburial.

I was flattered to be invited to the events, but my time commitments were tight. As much as I would have liked to have met the family and pay my respects to Edward S., I could not free myself for the day. I did receive a copy of the proceedings and through this media was able to be a part of the happenings. I was, after the story was made public, finally able to talk about the true facts of this case.

The case was to say the least very unusual. While this case was very involved and time-consuming in its unfolding, the fact that the correct bodies were finally linked with the correct families made a gratifying conclusion.

The Couple

Rarely were many of the couples under the services of the district office married. Even more rare was it to have the couples have a child. One such couple did marry and have a child. I remember coming into the district office early one morning, and the couple was there with their child. We gave assistance in caring for the child, but it became clear that they were not able to fully care for the child. After many attempts to have them raise the child, sadly it was mutually decided that the child would be put up for adoption. It was a difficult decision for the couple but one that ultimately was probably in the child's best interest.

Group Homes in Wood County

In January 1976, the Wood County Board of Mental Retardation applied to the State Department of Mental Retardation for three homes to house twenty-four people. One home was for ambulatory residents, and two were for nonambulatory. These were the first of several homes the Wood County board would open.

The project was proceeding as planned until it was brought forth that the location of the homes would be across the road from Wood Lane School. The other possibility for this land was that a jail may be located on the same eighty-acre site as the group homes. The point my office and central office made on the construction of the building on this proposed site was that the residential flavor must be present for state funds to be granted.

After much discussion and the donation of land in Portage, Ohio, it was decided to move the location of the homes to have a residential-type setting. This was a good example of a building project being turned around so that residents would have the opportunity to have an acceptable living environment. The homes opened around December 21, 1978.

Children Services

One of the more challenging group homes we dealt with was the residential care unit located on the grounds of the Lucas County Children Services Center on River Road in Maumee. The residential care unit was for people with severe mental retardation and had more than but less than sixty residents. Upon taking over the district manager position, I was approached by the new director, Bob Carson, to visit the facility. I went on a visit of the facility and during the process was introduced to the unit director. The director informed me that the funding was tight. That was not good news to me as I had few available beds to house the individuals. Together, we worked hard to come up with alternate funding. Several changes took place, and within a short period, we had solved the funding problem and my need to come up with alternate placements. It was a change in services that was able to accomplish all the factors that needed to be addressed and preserved the relationship between my office and Lucas County Children Services. A well-fostered relationship between the two organizations was essential to the success of this project.

Abolish the District Offices

This abolishment was to be one of the most trying times of my life. I had worked to have the proper educational and professional credentials and was about to finish my Ph.D., and an office I had worked in day and night to be successful was going to be abolished. This job was my dream job, the one that I enjoyed greatly. While my employees were promised other jobs, I wasn't sure it would happen. I had no idea where my future was going. Though I had planned the change the best I could, work began at least by the end of 1977 to replace the twelve district offices with six regional centers. The commissioner of mental retardation was not pleased with the district offices giving services to newly released residents from institutions. The discussions on the future of the district office were difficult and hard to face, especially when the district offices were doing well considering the circumstances under which they were operating.

The proposed change took its toll on the office. Personally, my health underwent many negative changes in terms of my sleep and metabolism. With treatment, I lost little time on the job. Dealing with losing my office and my staff was made more difficult as the reasons for the closure made little sense.

Community

Ohio Special Olympics

Basketball

While my career path had changed into administration, I still was able to keep my involvement in Special Olympics. The state basketball tournament in April 1976 provided me with the opportunity to use my referee skills. It is rewarding to see teams evenly matched play well after many hours of practice. Knowing that I was in on the ground floor of the Special Olympics is a very positive feeling.

Ohio Special Olympics Summer Games

For the number of years, the Summer Games have existed, I have had the privilege of being part of the festivities. The meals committee has been my special interest and responsibility. Serving over five thousand people in about a forty-five-minute period is rewarding. The summer of 1976 was a close call with one of the volunteers' children. We were in the hot tub near the pool at the Holiday Inn when suddenly, Ronda lost her hold on the side and went under in the four-foot-deep enclosure. Luckily, I saw her go under and was able to pull her out with very little effort. The poor child was coughing and gasping for air for a while. I was happy I was near and lucky enough to catch her with the first try of my hands.

CHAPTER 6

Northwest Ohio Developmental Center

The district office had been one of my dream jobs, and now twelve district offices had throughout the state been combined into six regional offices. I had been told by the commissioner of developmental disabilities that to advance to the regional commissioner office, it was necessary for me to become superintendent of a developmental center. I was familiar with the programs at both the Tiffin Developmental Center and NODC as my office was involved with placement in both these centers. I knew NODC located at 1101 South Detroit Avenue, which served the ten counties located in Northwest Ohio, well as I was responsible for the building of the center as well as the opening and placement of consumers into the center. With my district manager position eliminated, NODC superintendent position seemed like the best available job alternative in my career plans. I interviewed for the position with some other very competent applicants, and after the scores were tallied, I was the top contender. I was offered the position and accepted the offer. The challenges to be faced were to be more than I imagined, and the elements of success were always balanced by the possibility of defeat. This job was to be one of the greatest rides in my career as the opportunity unfolded for many to move from state facilities to community-based facilities and delivery systems.

A Marriage and a Kidnapping

An event occurred that I had never in my wildest dreams thought would happen to me. The date was June 6, 1980. My son Joey was the ring bearer for my neighbor girl Carol Welty and her husband-to-be, Jim Biddle, from Williamsburg, Pennsylvania. We were at the reception dinner at Kaufman's Restaurant in downtown Bowling Green. I received a call from the *Toledo Blade* near the end of the dinner, asking me as the superintendent of NODC for a statement on the young boy under my care who had been found in the Maumee River. I did not yet have information on this event but promised the *Toledo Blade* that I would get back to them in fifteen minutes. My heart sank. What had happened, and why hadn't I been contacted?

I called my program director and explained the call from the newspaper. I was told the eleven-year-old boy was playing outside the cottage after supper. He was under supervision and was playing in a grassy area surrounded by asphalt. He would not walk on asphalt. He was seen a few hours later by staff at a festival north of the facility. He was found crying near the shore of the Maumee River by a passing boat. The young boy didn't cross the street and couldn't talk.

The young boy was not known to run off and was being supervised from inside the cottage. An unauthorized person must have taken him off the grounds. He was found unharmed. That evening, I met with the parents and explained what had happened. To obtain more information, it was attempted to procure a federal agency such as the FBI. The only evidence we had was another resident who saw what happened, but this resident was without speech. No new information was obtained after this point, and the supervision procedure was changed in the cottage.

During the afternoon before the wedding, we were having a party in our yard with many of the people associated with the wedding. A tradition in rural Pennsylvania of stealing the bride was to take place in Ohio. Several of Jim's friends invaded our yard and stole Carol. It was a well-planned event! The wedding proceeded that day after the stolen bride was returned, and that evening, I spent most of my time at the reception talking to the media about the kidnapping.

Another Lawsuit

On the last year of my tenure at NODC, I was sitting in the human relations supervisor's office when I looked out the window toward the main highway, Detroit Avenue. As I peered out the window, I saw one of our vans hit two cars on Detroit Avenue. I looked further, and one of our residents was leaving the wrecked van. I recognized the resident and began to run out to the van as I was concerned that the resident might be hit while walking on this main highway. I was not the only person who heard the crash as the resident was under the care of a staff member before I was able to access the wreck. I found out that our resident had gone into the maintenance building, taken the key, started the van, and driven the van down the NODC boulevard into the car on Detroit Avenue.

I was at the scene for a few minutes when Steve, the chief of operations, informed me the wrecker was coming to tow the van. I asked Steve how long it would take for the wrecker to arrive on site, and he said a few minutes. I asked him to call the wrecker again and get the wrecker here now. I was concerned about the van being in the street and possibly causing more accidents. I was also concerned that live coverage by the media wouldn't do anyone at the center any good. With the new timeline of "right now" established, the wrecker came and picked up the car and left the site about one minute before the TV media was there, ready to shoot film. Changes were made immediately on the safe storage of vehicle keys.

The parents filed a lawsuit against me and the facility for improper supervision. It was dismissed as I remember.

A Fire and a Resident

One summer afternoon, I remembered receiving a call from one of the nearby residents of the center. It seems one our female residents had left the grounds and reentered her house. The resident had found a pack of matches and was lighting them when the neighbor reentered her home. She put out a small fire the resident had started in her ashtray. Fortunately, the resident was a cook at Larc Lane, a school for the developmentally disabled located a short distance from the center. The neighbor was understanding, and the resident was returned to the center.

Gerald Burkett

Gerald's family lived near Woodville. On weekends, Gerald liked to go home, so I would give him a ride to his home. Gerald's big event over the weekend was to go to an establishment in Woodville called Jo Jo's. His family would spend the evening there, and Gerald always talked of having a great time. When I picked Gerald up after the weekend to take him back to NODC, he would relate to me how much fun he had.

Another Couple

A couple located at the center were very close. They would at times leave the center together and explore the community. It became evident that they had reached the point in their lives where they were capable of independent living. They were released from the center and lived in the community. While the relationship had its ups and downs, they couple was successful in living in the community.

Another Job Opening

I was to interview and obtain the job I desired, the regional commissioner job. As part of my responsibility, I was to be responsible for both NODC and the Tiffin Developmental Center. Tiffin had been known as a sound mental health center and now a stable developmental center for the mentally retarded.

The approximately two years at NODC had been full of challenges. The staff members, other service providers, residents, parents, families, and community had grown to support me and the center.

I must recognize the most important other person in my life, the one I fall in love with each day of my life, my lovely wife, Kathy. She was always there to support me and share with me this very important part of my life. As I recognize Kathy, I would also like to recognize the other significant people of NODC employment, past and present. They supported me, and they have given more than I will ever know.

I read an unknown quote that best summarizes my experiences at NODC and some of my experiences yet to come. It went like this: "As we sail through life, don't avoid rough waters, sail on because calm waters won't make a skillful sailor."

Best of luck to the staff in the future and thank you for the pleasure of working with all of you.

CHAPTER 7

Regional Commissioner

The experiences at NODC had been challenging and helpful in my future years as a manager. When Walter Solarz decided to leave the regional commissioner position, I knew where I wanted to go. I had worked for Walt less than ten years ago and knew he would help me in my adjustment period. This position had been one of my dream jobs. There had been talk that the regional office could be done away with, but since most other state department systems had regional or district offices, it didn't make sense to do away with the regional offices. I was excited about the position, knew many of the major service providers, and therefore was anxious to obtain and guide the Region II Office in its growth.

The Role of the Regional Office

The role of the district office and the regional office had many similarities. Two of the big differences were that the regional office served a larger geographic area and was responsible for NODC and the Tiffin Developmental Center.

The Regional II office was in Toledo as part of the Ohio Department of MRDD. The office coordinated and monitored services for people with mental retardation and developmental disabilities for the nineteen counties in Northwest Ohio. One of the major functions of the office was to bring together a comprehensive regional plan composed of information contributed from each of the counties. By law, the county board of mental retardation was responsible to provide or contract for services for the MRDD population. Residential services had been provided by the state of Ohio in institutions, and then the focus changed to developmental centers so that residents were prepared to live in the community. The trend of living in one's home county had been ongoing for several years. The regional plan addressed needs, goals, objectives, and resources needed to obtain these goals and objectives as well as a definition of the present service delivery system. The Region II plan was combined into a state plan for the Department of MRDD. Residential planning was the area of big program growth and was therefore a large part of this regional and state plan.

The Region II Advisory Council

It was an exciting time to be involved in the program changes, especially in the residential area. Along with these exciting times were many challenges on how the needs of the MRDD population were going to be met. For example, if a residential home was needed in the county, where were the funds going to be found? Another question was who was going to provide these services? The county board or a contract agency? The Region II Advisory Council provided direction to the Region II staff and the region. This council was a wide-range representation from community residential facilities, county boards, Association for Retarded Citizens, workshops, developmental centers, Ohio Private Residential Association, and area universities. Their guidance was invaluable in helping answer these questions and others such as expansion in multiple areas. A new residential placement in the area meant the need for a new workshop or community job placement with the other expenses that go with living in the community.

The Region II Advisory Board had committees in the public relations, planning, finance, residential, and program. These committees addressed issues pertinent to funding, eligibility for services, residential development, planning, objectives, media communications, and many other issues.

Residential Development and Implementation, Funding, Monitoring, Licensure, and Evaluation

At this time, there were ninety-one licensed community residential facilities often funded by the Department of MRDD, serving over 650 residents and eight intermediate care facilities for the mentally retarded (ICF/MR), largely funded by the federal government, serving over three hundred people, plus two developmental centers under the direct control of the Region II office. Tiffin Developmental Center had 220 residents, and NODC had 170 residents, with a mix of private, state, and federal funding. These facilities enabled the intake and placement staff of the regional office to identify appropriate placements in the community on a twenty-four-hour period. The calls for residential placements came at all times of the day and night, so the twenty-four-hour on call was accurate.

At this time, most of the nineteen counties had some type of residential home. The law required the provision of the most appropriate, least restrictive environment, and that type of placement might not be available in each county, so available placement might be required in another county in the state. With the advantage of serving all nineteen counties as well as contacts with the other five regions and the developmental centers, a placement was needed to be identified within a short period. The developmental center closest to the county of residence would become the last option.

The placement of a person from one county into another was not always an easy matter. A new person placed into a county different from where they were previously living was an additional expenditure in day programming for the new county.

In each regional office, there was a residential development specialist who searched for potential home operators, discussed the available funding and license requirements, and identified with the case managers the client(s) who were eligible and available for placement into the home.

Another essential section that was housed in the Region II office provided expertise for the over ninety homes. The license specialists and monitors did initial an annual review and quarterly monitor of the homes licensed by the Department of MRDD.

Fiscal Department

In Region II during this time, there were $8.5 million of purchase of service funds within the nineteen county areas. During fiscal years 1983, 1984, and 1985, it was projected that $14 million of purchase of service would be converted to federal Medicaid funds. This would convert to several millions of dollars savings to the state. Only through close monitoring, consultation, and coordination would these conversions take place. The Region II office would be involved with these changes to ensure the use of purchase of services in other residential development.

Monitoring and Evaluation of Educational and Workshop Programs

Housed within the Region II office were program consultants. These consultants were responsible for ensuring that the rules and regulations of the MRDD as well as other state and federal regulations are met. The consultants ensure the flow of educational and transportation state funds to the county boards. As a result of the flow of information from the state to the county, the program consultants provide ideas in the program delivery system.

Case Management

At this time, the regional offices provided the case management services to all people living within the state-funded and ICF/MR Medicaid–funded homes. It was recommended that the case management within the regional office be contracted with the county boards of MRDD while a small core of case managers in the regional office managed these contracts. In a survey counting all moderate, severe, and profound people with mental retardation in the nineteen counties served by the Region II office, it was recommended that on a 1:300 ratio, at least twenty-seven case managers and case manager supervisors were needed. The role of case management was to be a major discussion area as systems changed in the next few years, one I would be having a different and major role in very soon.

In-Service

Because of the ever-changing state and federal legislation and the need for in-services in administration, program, fiscal, and legal area, a staff development, and training task force consisting of twenty-five members met monthly to assess and plan regional programs. The task force had representation from a variety of area educational programs, resource organizations, and providers of MRDD services. A few of the training sessions were on such topics as human sexuality, Title XX, guardianship, client programming, and other state and federal funding.

More on the Role of Regional Commissioner

Media

When anything of importance happened at the regional office, the media was somehow notified, and the results were reported in the paper. Dealing with the media was an ongoing task requiring much time and expertise to properly present the facts.

Winter Traveling

Going to and from Columbus provided me with many interesting travel experiences. I will share one instance involving a trip to a meeting in Tiffin. After the meeting, I was to travel to Columbus for another meeting. I do not remember the purpose of either meeting, but I do remember the trip from Tiffin to Columbus.

It was winter, and there had been an ice storm the night before. Shortly after I had left Tiffin, I approached a hill in the road. As I slowed down, the car turned sideways, and before I could react, I found myself on the right side of the road in the front yard of a house. A mailbox was on my left side, and the home was on my right. I had probably ten feet of clearance on each side of the car. I also noted that the ice was breaking, and there was snow beneath the ice. Since I didn't know how deep the snow was and was afraid of getting stuck and the path ahead of me was clear, I did not try to stop the car and probably couldn't.

I successfully passed several more houses on the right and mailboxes and newspaper holders on the left. I was looking for lawn ornaments in my path and a break from the mail and newspaper boxes on my left. Like a miracle, I saw an opening that led to the road with nothing blocking my path. I looked for any traffic on the road and turned my wheel to the left and gave it a little gas so my rear end would help me turn left. The car turned left and started up a slight incline. As I began to reach the road, I turned to the right again, gave it a little gas, and was on the road. I stabilized the car by straightening the steering wheel. I slowed down to a crawl and regained my composure. As I reviewed my experience in the front yard of several residents living on this road, I immediately realized I was very lucky to have come through this incident without a scratch on me or my car. I felt that a force higher than me aided in helping me manage this circumstance.

To Mount Vernon, Ohio, Developmental Center

At this time, there was a hearing on one of the residential homes in my area. I had enlisted the help of other superintendents to conduct the hearing. On the way down to Mount Vernon, I had a huge gas attack. I looked for a gas station so I could relieve the pressure. I found a restroom and was going to make it until I found the restroom door was locked. I didn't make it safely to the restroom but was able to contain the runny bowel movement in my underwear. I threw away the underwear and was able to clean myself up. I arrived at the hearing on time, and this is the first public statement on how I made it to the hearing in a presentable manner.

Capital Construction

From the time I began working for the state of Ohio, I was involved in building or renovating several residential homes, workshops, and schools. A total of nine schools, thirteen residential homes, and three workshops bringing several million dollars to Northwest Ohio was obtained. Another state project costing $8.2 million resulted in NODC, which served counties.

Regional Office to Be Abolished

Richard Celeste was elected governor of Ohio on November 3, 1982. Abolishing the regional office was now a reality. On February 22, 1983, I was asked to submit a letter of resignation. I submitted my resignation and was fortunate to obtain another job in the department.

Several months earlier, I began to have a chemical imbalance in my body. I received help and was back on the job within two weeks.

CHAPTER 8

Impact Grants Coordinator

The regional offices throughout the state of Ohio had been abolished. While there was nothing, I knew I had done to affect the office's elimination, I was still without a job. A new wave of closing state facilities and having residents placed in the community was a new reality. While residents had been placed in the past into the community, there were more challenging residents who were now to be placed. Since my credentials were very strong in programs for the mentally retarded and I had worked with many of the superintendents of county boards of mental retardation and developmental disabilities, I was offered the job of impact grants coordinator. The job was to place residents, primarily from Orient Developmental Center south of Columbus, into day programs preferably in their home counties. While the placement of people into a county required food, clothing, and a home to live in, the provision of rehabilitation or habilitation services was essential. My job was to specifically work with the county boards to use existing placements, help find new facilities or placements, and see that program funds flowed to these newly placed residents and their counties of origin.

At this time, Orient was for sure being converted into a prison; there was also talk of other developmental centers such as Apple Creek being converted into a prison. The other happening at this time was developing group homes in the community. Several communities were opposed to group homes in their neighborhood. One reason was that property values would decrease. Property values did not decrease.

One interesting factor was whether the community be involved in the development of the group home, or since it might be seen as a right of the mentally retarded to live in the community, they could be established without asking for special permission.

Another criticism is that people were moved too fast out of the institutions to community homes without proper staff training. The original date to close Orient was December 1983. Because of court actions, the last resident moved out on April 12, 1984.

As people moved into the community, there were accusations of not enough monitoring of the new community residents from developmental centers by case managers who did the monitoring.

A Trip to Dayton

One of the residential centers with less than one hundred residents was in Dayton, Ohio. The center was largely funded by my department. A meeting was set for seven o'clock on this morning and I left from home around three o'clock in the morning. There were between ten and twenty people at the meeting. Many issues were discussed about the funding and operation of the center. Fortunately, the meeting went well, and I stayed to meet some of the residents and staff. Some of the unusual happenings of the residents such as leaving the center and not returning were addressed. The center was well run and an example for the rest of the state on how to maintain a center.

Celebrating My Doctorate

I was approaching my fortieth birthday and had finished my requirements for the PhD. We celebrated with a Mass at St. Thomas More Parish in Bowling Green. The Mass was a thank-you to the several people involved in helping me reach this goal. We had a luncheon to top off the memorable day.

A New Position

A position opened in central office, and I was asked to move to Columbus and take over the management of the case management system for the entire state of Ohio.

CHAPTER 9

Chief of State Case Management

With so many residents being moved from state developmental centers to their counties of origin and with existing residents of various facilities such as group homes having many needs, the staff person responsible to see the plans for the provision of all services was the case management specialist. Every county had at least one and larger counties several case managers to overlook the long-term and short-term everyday needs of people with mental retardation and developmental disabilities. One afternoon in early January, Director Minnie Johnston called me into her office and informed me that I would be responsible for 184 employees in each of the counties in the state of Ohio. Some case managers were employed directly on the state payroll, and others were employed by the counties. Regardless of employment, I was to provide the direction and rules for this statewide system. One of my major goals was to see that all the responsibility for managing the case managers switched to the counties.

I held a meeting of all case managers early in my tender. There were over one hundred case managers, and I held the meeting in Columbus to outline how case management was to shift from the state to the county. The shift took place after much work by me and others.

Shortly thereafter, at three o'clock one afternoon, I was informed that the administrative rule for case management was to be presented to the governor the next day. I had started on the rule, but it was not complete. I arose around three in the morning the next day and went into the central office in downtown Columbus to finish the rule. The guard at the office was not going to allow me in the building until I told him I was completing a report for the governor and he could tell the governor I couldn't enter the building. I finished the rule, and it was retyped and sent to the governor that day.

I was living full time in Columbus.

Case Management Services
A Few Cases

Each day had many various happenings in Ohio, and many times, I had to direct case managers on how to handle the cases as the buck stopped with me. The following are a few of those cases that I and my staff had to directly deal with.

Water Burn

In one northwestern county, a mentally retarded adult was taking a bath. The water temperature was scalding, and the aide placed the person into the water. The individual was burned and later died of complications.

Man Stabbed Lady

I was walking to work one early morning crossing the Veterans Bridge in Columbus when I received a call that a case manager in the county of residence was entering a courtroom where a mentally retarded man was being charged with attempted murder. The case manager asked me what she should do. I said to ask for a new date or continuance so we could prepare a defense case. The continuance was granted.

The background information was that the young man had previously received a check for social security. He had met a young lady who was friendly with him, and he gave her his check. The girl he stabbed reminded him of the lady who had received his check.

Young Girl in Chair Choked Herself to Death

I was reviewing an unusual incident that had been sent to the state. All major unusual incidents in the entire state had to be reported to my office in Columbus. A girl was in a chair and had slipped down, causing her to choke on one of the straps that held her in the chair. I called in one of my assistants and told her to call this home immediately and have the resident placed in a different, safer chair. As I was giving instructions to my assistant, another assistant came in and said the same girl had slipped again and had choked to death.

Three Brothers and Sister

I remember one call that came in where there were three adults with developmental disabilities living in a house with their elderly mother. How elderly was the mother? Very elderly and very sick. She needed an operation and had no resources to take care of the three offspring. My caseworkers had evaluations done immediately, and as quick, homes were found for the three adults so that the mother could have her operation. Successfully handling this type of situation is why social services exist.

Exit Report

Later in the year, I was to leave this position so I could take a position closer to home. I was to prepare a large notebook on all the areas that needed attention in my area of responsibility. A large document was prepared that contained many areas that were in process. One of these areas was not followed up on by an assigned attorney. The attorney lost her job because of her inactions.

PART III

A Second and Third Chance with the County and Bowling Green State University (BGSU)

CHAPTER 10

Wood County Director of Day Services and Director of Special Projects

At this time in my career, I was ready to leave the state system and obtain a job where I could live with my family and work nearby. Working in Columbus as the director of case management for Ohio had been a more than challenging position with responsibilities in each of the eighty-eight counties. I had located various superintendent jobs around the state and was originally planning to apply for them. When I talked over my options with my wife and two sons, I found that they had ideas different from mine. The major difference between their plans and mine was that they all three wished to stay in Wood County. Kathy had lived in Wood County for fifteen years and really preferred to stay in the area. My son, Joe, was in close reach of high school and was not fond of leaving the area as was my youngest son, Mark. Each of them had their friends and didn't wish to leave the area.

I, on the other hand, did not have a job possibility close to our present home and needed to find a job in the area. I had for the past several years been in CEO-type positions that were responsible for many employees

79

and the services to many consumers. I had the experience, and I had my PhD in educational administration and supervision. Working with other people, I have been told, is a major strength of mine. I was in the middle of making a very difficult decision. What seemed best for me was to move, though my family didn't necessarily agree with me. I spent many hours trying to come up with a decision where everyone would be happy. I used any energy that I could muster from my unborn twin, my God, and my reserve energy source; and then I went back and tried to find more energy. In the meantime, I had my position in Columbus and could buy some time until other options might develop.

I really didn't know what to do but pray. It worked; finally, I heard that there was to be a position created in Wood County called the assistant superintendent/director of day services. I have for years known many employees from the Wood County board. In several of my former jobs with the state of Ohio, I had grown to know the administration and several employees who were none other than top-notch professionals. They say that you can tell the organization by its leader. I have already talked about Ray Anderson and his wife, Betty. Ray's leadership lasted until 1976 when he became the superintendent of NODC. Ray was succeeded by Douglas McVey, who had been a longtime business associate working with me and others to start the Ohio Athletic Association for the Mentally Retarded in the early 1970s, which became the Ohio Special Olympics. Doug and his wife, Ann, had been acquaintances of ours for years, and the position had many pluses.

Since I first worked in Richland and Lucas counties, a lapse of twelve years had taken place. While working for MRDD, I was working with the same population and the funding and the manner of delivering service was different. The state was more monitoring of services; and in at least one job, the superintendent of NODC, the emphasis was on a particular population rather than all populations in my area of responsibility. Since the service and delivery of service was changing, a look at these areas from the year 1985 seems warranted.

The jobholder in this new position was responsible for many facets of the program's operations. In addition to being responsible for the superintendent in his absence, it was responsible for over one hundred employees in the following departments: the Wood Lane School under the supervision of Caroline Dene, the Wood Lane Adult Services with Dr. John Roberts at the helm, Community Employment Services (CES) conducted by Bill Clifford, Special Olympics led by Mary Sehmann, community resources with Liz Sheets, food services headed by Sonja Hammer, transportation with Linda Donley, and maintenance and grounds managed by Mark Carpenter.

I applied and was chosen for the position. While this position was to be one of the most challenging of my career, it was also to be done with another group of truly professional people.

Robert, My Friend

I had grown to know one of the people working in the sheltered workshop named Robert Smithers. He had lived in northern Wood County his entire life. I was to have him as a special friend and spent time with him every few weeks.

On one of those weekends, he had wanted to return to where he had lived before moving to one of the group homes in Wood County. We went back to where he'd lived previously and began to visit people he had known in his younger days. Everyone we went to see remembered Robert, and we had a great time talking to his many friends. It was amazing how popular Robert was and how happy all were to see Robert.

Robert would come to our house and visit with Kathy, Joe, Mark, and me. One of Robert's favorite activities was to drive our riding lawn mower under my supervision. He would have driven the mower for hours if he had his way.

He had known Gene Walston, our neighbor, and loved to visit Gene and his farm. On one occasion Gene was combining and Robert rounded the field many times with Gene. This event provided the cover picture for 5this book. On another occasion in the evening, he persuaded one of the group home supervisors to take him to Gene's house for a visit.

Robert was good friends of one of my neighbors, Bob Pugh. Bob was a farmer and lived a few miles from our home. Bob had passed away, and we would visit his grave in Fish Cemetery. Over the years, Robert had developed his own form of language. He would say Bob's name and point down to the earth and up to heaven. That meant that Bob had died and went to heaven. If he said "morrow," that would mean tomorrow. "Morrow, morrow" would mean two days away. If he would say Joe and laugh, he meant that Joe was funny.

One afternoon, I took Robert to Julie and Eric Getz's house to see Bob's former residence. The visit was a great experience for Robert and hopefully the Getz's.

Robert fell sick, and it was a sad day when he passed. He had many friends, and they all would miss him. This is the Robert in the title of this book!

Elvis Presley and Tommy

One of the adults in the program lived in Bloomsdale, Ohio. His name was Tommy, and he had a great collection of Elvis memorabilia. I had a meeting at his house one evening and saw the many animals that he had collected over the years. I especially remember the birds, one being a golden pheasant. Tommy showed me his room, which was filled with Elvis records, scarves, and other of Elvis's collectibles. While his parents were active in the Wood Lane program, they wished Tommy to stay home as long as possible. This was and is a very common practice.

John from Grand Rapids

John's parents were from Grand Rapids, Ohio. John was a true redhead man and was a person with Down syndrome. John always had a smile, and his parents were very proud of their only son. John loved sports and was involved in the Special Olympics program.

Francis Gannon

Francis was the switchboard operator and handled all the calls into the program. Francis lived with her sister and brother-in-law in Bowling Green. Francis was involved in Special Olympics and was one of the several people I used to speak in my classes at BGSU. Francis was a good example of a person who could hold a full-time job in Wood County. Dave Miller, a board member, had lobbied for a person to work in the program; and Francis turned out to be that person. After Francis moved away, another person from the program took her place, and that tradition is still present in the program.

Monica Roth

One of the most tragic experiences I was involved with was on Monday, March 14, 1988. I was returning from a trip to Columbus, and upon arriving in Bowling Green, I was informed that there had been an accident involving a bus from Wood Lane. One of the large buses had gone off the right side of a country road, and the driver overcorrected. Unfortunately, the bus driver lost control of the bus and it flipped. One of the students, Monica Roth, was killed. Many others were injured.

As the person responsible for transportation, I and many of the other administrators were to spend many hours following up on the accident with local state and federal authorities. The publicity around this tragedy lasted for some time after the accident. The parents of the child were to suffer the loss of their only child. It was a loss I was not to understand until Kathy and I were to lose our son Mark many years later. The news coverage was constant even in the mass of burial Thursday in the Good Shepherd Catholic Church in Toledo.

A formal investigation into the accident was required by the National Transportation Safety Board. I was assigned the task of preparing every minute detail of the wreck in a formal report. The result was a very thick book, which was submitted to the authorities. A lesson we all learned was that you can never be careful enough in protecting the lives of our students and adults.

Mike Nichols

Another employee in the sheltered workshop was Mike. Mike always had a smile on his face and was a joy to be around. Mike's family were very strong supporters of the Wood County Board of Developmental Disabilities. They were to provide the land for three group homes in Portage, one being the Nichols Home. They also donated funds for the Nichols Therapy Pool in Bowling Green.

Mike passed on April 5, 2022. The following paragraph was submitted by me through the Maison-Dardenne-Walker Funeral Home in Maumee on May 19, 2022.

"I was honored to know Mike and his many positive ways. The Nichols family of Mike, his father John, his mother Nancy, and his sister Susan will be remembered for their many contributions to Wood Lane. The Nichols Home and the Nichols Therapy Pool were two of the many ways in which the family will be known forever. It was a pleasure for me to be involved in both these projects."

Richard Layman

One of the families had three offspring in the program. Mary and Richard were devoted parents to their sons and daughter and were constantly advocating for better services for them.

Their only daughter, Phyllis, was in the adult program and lived at home. Their older son, Charlie, was employed in the program as a maintenance worker. He worked in the school and was an excellent employee. He also lived at home. I believe he retired from that position. Their second son, James, worked in the sheltered workshop and lived in one of the group homes.

I remember going to the parent's funerals and was always touched by the tireless efforts that they and many of the other parents I had known put into making sure that the best possible programs were provided for their sons and daughters.

Another Family

Another family had two men who were employees of the sheltered workshop. One of them, Robert, would always stop me when I was going through the workshop and say, "Hey, buddy!" He would reach out his hand and make my day as he would give me a great big handshake. Later, he was to work in the garage washing the buses and cars owned by the program. This was another program where the board would make jobs for the adults in the program. The supervisor of this program worked for many years making sure that vehicles were scheduled and well cleaned. There are so many dedicated workers in this field that I could never do justice to their many unselfish efforts to improve the lives of those entrusted to our care. Thanks to all of you!

A Final Family

A family that I was to have a long-term relationship with was the Bosch family. Ray and Mary Jo Bosch were the parents, and they had several sons and daughters who helped with Special Olympics at the State Summer Games in Columbus. One of the sons, Dennis, I see often at our church.

Christy, their daughter, was an exceptional young lady who was born with Down syndrome. While active in several Special Olympics sports, she was also manager of the basketball team at one of the local high schools. Christy lived to see her thirty-fourth birthday; and after her passing, she was honored by having a restaurant established in her name, Christy's Corner Cafe, located at 368 Rice Street in Elmore, Ohio 43416. The major employees of the cafe are individuals with developmental disabilities. The purpose of the restaurant is the following: *"YOUR SUPPORT WILL ENABLE US TO IMPROVE THE FUTURE OF PEOPLE WITH DISABILITIES BY PROVIDING MEANINGFUL JOB OPPORTUNITIES. HELP US REACH OUR GOAL OF $50,000."* The website is christyscornercafe.com

Come and enjoy a great meal!

Richard and Kit

When I first came into the program, there was one individual that I remember worked in the community. That person was Richard, and he worked as a bagger at the local Kroger. As I best remember, Jerry Pearl was the workshop director and he was involved in helping Richard become a worker at Kroger. Richard had a lady friend named Julie, and I remember seeing them in the community. Richard was another of the many people who would come to my classes at BGSU and tell his story to the many students I had the pleasure of instructing. I often see Richard when I have dinner meetings for a group called Griefshare at the senior center in Bowling Green.

Another Kroger employee who was to be a stock person was Kit. He worked for several years at Kroger, and his mother and father always supported him in any way possible. Whenever I would go into Kroger, Kit would always come over to me and make sure I could find what I needed to find in his department. This personal approach was always appreciated.

John Beck

John and his family were very active in the program. His daughter started as a student in the school, and his son was in public school. He and his wife were involved in the ARC (Association for Retarded Citizens and John served as president. John was also a member of the Wood County Board of Developmental Disabilities and gave many years in service to that organization. John served with Dick in the maintenance department at BGSU. I could always count on John for his support!

Tim Bomeli

Tim was an employee of Uhlman's, a clothing store in Bowling Green. Tim's father, an accountant, and was for years on the local board and spent hours making sure that Wood Lane had the resources to provide some of the best services in the state. I was a little biased in my belief.

Tim's job was to clean the store, and he held that position for many years. His presence allowed people to be in contact with persons with disabilities, and Tim's smile reinforced that positive image. Tim loved Special Olympics and was ever present in that program.

Lisa Sipes

Lisa was the only child of Ted and Jo. Ted was a college professor and spent many years advocating for persons with disabilities. He was also one of the unpaid editors of my first book. Unfortunately, his medical problems got too severe, and he was to lose his fight for life. Jo survived both Lisa and Ted and after her professional career as a teacher was to continue to be a strong advocate for the disabled. She served with me for years on the Special Olympics Advisory Board in Wood County.

Lisa was a most unusual lady. With the support of her parents, she was to own her own house and lived independently with her white cat. Lisa was employed for years at Kentucky Fried Chicken. An avid bocce player and participant in other Special Olympics, she was to compete at the Ohio State games on many occasions. Like her parents, she was one of the several volunteers who would serve meals for many years at the state games.

Lisa was also a torchbearer in Bowling Green when the law enforcement personnel would run the torch from several cities in Ohio to the Summer Games in Columbus to raise money for Special Olympics. Lisa was a very busy person and always found time to be one of the participants in my classes at BGSU. Their memory lives on as the bocce courts at Wood Lane were to be named in their honor.

Jolynn Joyce

Jolynn was another adult who worked in the program. She worked for years in the kitchen at the school and was a server and did many other jobs in that capacity. She always had a smiling face and was involved in the Special Olympics program. Her sister was always an advocate for her.

Recently, I was outside doing some work in my yard and saw Jolynn approaching my property. She was with a relative who was having her taxes done at one my neighbors. It was a pleasant experience for me to renew our friendship.

Larry Hampton

Larry was a very large man and worked in the sheltered workshop. Larry always met you with a smile. His parents were active in the program and always were interested in seeing that Larry was getting the best services possible.

Leland LeBay

Leland worked in the workshop. His father lived in the country and invited Kathy and me there to pick some of his wild berries.

Leland was always in the annual talent show put on by the residential services program. In the talent show, individuals were involved in skits or displayed their talents. Leland was a guitar player and loved to lead the crowd in some of his many songs. The talent show was held usually at the mall in Bowling Green and always played to a packed house.

Ginger Donley

Ginger was a very pleasant girl in the workshop. Her parents were active as parents. Her father, Larry, was employed in the program as a maintenance person; and her mother, Linda, was head of the transportation department.

David Schult

David was one of the first students in Wood Lane School. He was a tall thin man in the sheltered workshop. His mother, Gladys, was the first classroom aid in the school; and his father, Henry, helped procure the first car to carry the students. Later, she graduated from Bowling Green Normal School (BGSU). The Schult group home in Bowling Green is named after her.

The first teacher at the school was Phyllis Dunn, a relative of the owners of Dunn Funeral Home in Bowling Green, Ohio.

Mary Restle

Mary was another of the first students at the school. Her parents, Bernadine and Chuck, were among the first parents to start Wood Lane School. I would run into Chuck at many of the district Boy Scout events as he was on the district committee.

Bob Jones

Bob was another of the first students in the school I knew. He lived around the corner from our first house near Lucky. We would see his mother, Boots, often in the yard doing outdoor activities.

The ARC

The Association for Retarded Citizens was an organization in Ohio, which had a chapter in many of its counties. I was to have the honor of representing the program as a staff representative. Each year, the organization would sponsor events. They would raise money through events such as the annual walk/run contest and spend the proceeds for a variety of the needs of the program.

Judy Hines was another parent who was the treasurer and president of the ARC. Judy's daughter, Julie, was an employee of the sheltered workshop. The hours that Judy gave to the ARC and the program were exceptional by any standard. Julie's father Maurice (Moe) was also active as a parent. These parent organizations were the initial movements in providing the energy to start the many programs that evolved into the county boards. Never underestimate the power of parents! Whenever I needed a few bucks for a special program, ARC was always there.

Leaving

I enjoyed working in the Wood County Board of DD for fifteen years. I was to be involved in many programs for the disabled and served on many unique programs to benefit them and the general population of the county. I retired from public employment, but immediately came out of retirement to serve as Superintendent of the Henry County Board of DD, another position that was to challenge my management skills.

CHAPTER 11

The Doctoral Degree and Teaching at BGSU

Completing the Doctor of Philosophy Degree (PhD)

To be a professor and teach on your own credentials, it is necessary in the departments I was to be teaching (Educational Administration and Supervision and Special Education) to have a PhD. In 1984, I was granted the Doctor of Philosophy from the Department of Educational Administration and Supervision at BGSU. Dr. Bill Reynolds was my advisor.

The journey lasted many years with many changes in the process. In 1970, I began my work on my PhD. In 1974, I completed my specialist degree in Educational Administration and Supervision. The specialist degree is earned after the master's degree and before the PhD. The major purpose I had in obtaining the specialist degree was to protect the many courses I had already taken for the PhD. If I didn't receive the specialist degree, all the courses I had taken between 1970 and 1974 might have to be taken again as the courses were not protected. The specialist degree protected or "saved" the courses so they would count for the PhD even if the timelines on the courses were not met. There were reasons other than coursework at that time why I could not complete my PhD. At that time, there was a requirement for a doctoral student to take a foreign language. I saw no reason for taking a foreign language. I would have also needed to quit working and go to school full time as a graduate student. I could not give up my job as I was supporting a family, and once one gives up a job, what assurance do they have that they will be able to obtain that job or another job?

With the specialist degree, I had my courses protected and hoped that there would be a change in both these areas so that I could finish the PhD. Within a few years, I found that the requirement that a PhD student would need to go to classes full time and not work wasn't still in place. The requirement that I was to take a language still stood, but computer science was now one of the options. Computer science was a language that was to be useful to me the rest of my life. One can see that change was essential in many areas for me to ultimately reach my educational goals.

Teaching at BGSU

For approximately ten years in the late 1980s and early 1990s, I had the pleasure of teaching at BGSU in the two departments I have mentioned. In those years, I usually taught one night a week for two to three hours. I taught such courses as introduction to special needs people, mental retardation, employment of the handicapped, and human resources. While I was reimbursed for teaching, the reimbursement was not significant. Adjunct professors are paid according to a contract and therefore do not have status as an employee of the university. In the beginning years of teaching, there were around twelve students. As time moved on, the small classroom was converted into a huge lecture hall, and seventy-five-plus students with no graduate assistant was the norm. Each of these students was paying several hundred dollars for each course in which they were enrolled. Since the adjunct professor would be receiving a few thousand dollars per course, significant money was to be made by the university. With my PhD, I was able to teach on my own credentials.

Making the classroom as real of an experience as possible was easy because I had several people who loved to come to my class and participate. This included both staff and my many friends who were enrollees of the program. This allowed staff to explain the many programs offered by the local program and gave them an opportunity to reach future employees.

The many enrollees over the years who visited my class were proud of their jobs and lives, and it gave students a chance to see that people with disabilities could be employed in a variety of jobs and could answer any questions they had about their daily lives.

I never had a problem finding adults to come to my class and share their lives. If anything, I was not able to have everyone who wished to participate be present. I tried to give every person a chance to present in my class. I am happy to say that I believe the students always enjoyed these presentations, and I know the presenters did a great job and enjoyed the experience. As they say, a great fit for all!

One of the classes I taught for years dealt with employment of the disabled. When I left Wood Lane, there were more than 199 people employed in the community. What a tribute to the staff and the people employed in the community.

While at Wood Lane, I had the honor of being on and presiding over the Special Education Advisory Board. This was a board comprised of people in the field who offered guidance to the Special Education Department. Ed Fiscus was for years head of the department and worked with this board. The Department of Rehabilitation also had an advisory board, and I represented Wood Lane on that board. Dr. Robert McGuffy was head of that department.

CHAPTER 12

Henry County Board of Developmental Disabilities

After thirty-five years of public service, most of which was in developmental disabilities, I decided to formally retire through the state's public employee retirement system. At the same time, I had procured a position as the superintendent of the Henry County Board of Developmental Disabilities, also known as Hope Services. I accepted this position because I was not ready to stop working at fifty-seven years of age, and I enjoyed the challenge of a superintendent or CEO position. Also, there is a financial advantage to this move.

I was aware that the position with the Henry County Board as with any county board at that time was to be challenging. I expected that this job would be like any other position I had held; if things were to go any way, it would be the hard way. I also knew that a big key to success in my tenure would be a positive relationship with the board, the staff, the consumers and their families, and the community. The changes coming down the line would require a board and staff to think of others and act as a team. If I was receiving energy from God and my twin, it would be needed because the economics alone would be one of the most taxing, if not the most taxing, undertakings in the job.

Why was the fiscal part of the job to be so difficult? The budget was very tight. At this time, the funding base of Medicaid for the residential program was being substituted for the existing funding base. This meant that continual change in terms of expenses and income would be constantly varying with what the federal government would allow. Other changes on programs, staff, and community perception would produce more challenges than the board, staff, or I could imagine. Much of the change just happened and cannot be explained on a rational basis because that is the way change is in government, federal in this case, and it cannot easily be predicted. It has been said that the product of government is many times like the process of making sausage. What the input into the sausage looks like and what the product looks like are two different-looking items.

The Henry County Board of Mental Retardation and Developmental Disabilities served 400 to 550 people, depending on which people were included. The services offered were some of the best I have ever seen in Ohio.

Staff

The staff professionals who work with children and adults in habilitation or training have certification requirements that must be met. Habilitation is accomplishing new skills that had not been learned before, while rehabilitation is accomplishing skills that had been present before.

Students and Adult Enrollees

School Age

The many stories I heard about individuals who were in the preschool program and had changed their lives around early w staggering.

I remember one public official tell me that his son had attended the preschool, and because of the socialization and training received, he had been able to attend a public school and have a very profitable future. This would not have been possible without this training. This person was to, on many occasions, give me support to carry out many positive goals for the program. This is just one of several success stories from the preschool.

Since the preschool had a mixture of disabled and regular students, each was to profit from exposure to each other. The program had the support of all the school districts and a great support of the community.

The students in the school program were now served in the public schools. Many of the students were involved in the Special Olympics program offered by Henry County.

Adult Services

Adult programs included a choice of employment programs called supported employment in the community or employment in a sheltered workshop in Stryker, Ohio, called Quadco. A senior program that offers a wide variety of recreational and educational programs is available at the Hope Services building in Napoleon.

Will Yeager

I first met Will's father, Ed, at a meeting when I was educational consultant for the state. We had a misunderstanding, and I spent the large part of a day with his parents straightening out this situation. At the time, Will's father was mayor of Napoleon or just out of office. Will's three others brothers were extremely dedicated to his future. The parents were very involved in starting the Henry County Board. Will was in the adult program in Henry County, and he had strong self-esteem. He thoroughly enjoyed his family and its activities. The family made arrangements for

Will to stay in his home with services provided by the Henry County Board.

Vanessa Lanzer

The Lanzer family was well-known in the Napoleon area as Mel, Vanessa's father, had started a construction company. His daughter Char was active in the business, and the Lanzer family was active in the Henry County Board.

Vanessa was a participant in the adult program.

Gwen Meyers

Gwen was in the adult program and a resident of one of the group homes. Her father, John, was a finance person in one of the local quarry businesses and was an extremely active board member in the Henry County Board of Developmental Disabilities.

Special Olympics

The Special Olympics program in Henry County was one of the best. It had grown and served the many people in the program and in the community, due largely to people such as Randy Barnes. Basketball was a very big part of the program. I remember one year we were going to a tournament, and our star player was bringing too much attention to himself and not being enough of a team player. We had talked it over, and it was my decision whether he would play or not. Being the one who wanted to give people the benefit of the doubt, I decided that he should play against the recommendation of some others.

The decision was based on the idea that he would be more of a team player and listen to the coach. The big game came, and the player could have done a better job in being a team player. I had given him the benefit of the doubt, and we lost the game with the player doing things more his way than the way we had agreed. You cannot win them all, and that is the way it goes. I tried!

Leaving

When the job is not as much fun, it is time to consider moving on. Five challenging years caused me to look closely at where I wanted to go with my time and life. Publishing some books had been weighing on me heavily because there was so much to do and, yes, so little time. I felt the Henry County program was in many ways better than when I came, and in others, there was still much work to be done.

I had promised myself to stay four to five years, and this was my fifth year. I and many others had done what we could to improve the program, and that is all that one can be expected to accomplish. In times of severe change, it is many times much more work than one anticipated or had time to accomplish. That was the case in Henry County, and I knew it was time to move on to the next challenge. The past must be the past because to try and relive it often is to cheat the present and future out of valuable time and attention.

PART IV

Retirement Experience

CHAPTER 13

Retirement Years

Retirement proved to have many activities not originally planned by Kathy or me. I had some plans to write books, and we had planned to do some remodeling of the house. The time required for the books, and for sure the time required to remodel the house, was many times the planned time. In addition, there was time for our newly formed church, St. John XXIII; time for my various extracurricular activities; and time for my family. Each day of the week had its own challenges like those I experienced when I was working.

Why Am I Tired?

In June of 2008, my son Mark and I were returning from the Ohio Special Olympics Summer Games in Columbus where my family and others were responsible to provide meals for the participating athletes and their coaches and chaperones. The largest number of meals served was at lunch on Saturday in which five thousand people were offered lunch. My day on Saturday started at around six o'clock for breakfast and ended after six o'clock supper with meals provided by Ohio State Food Services. Since our group usually enjoyed some evening activities, the weekend was not a time to catch up on one's sleep, so I was usually dragging after three days and three nights.

As Mark and I were traveling home on Route 23, I suddenly became very tired and began to doze off. I didn't doze off for long because my car drifted into the median, and the terrain was anything but smooth. I worked my way back to the road, giving Mark a bumpy road. This was the first time in recent years that I had dozed off, so I decided that with two occasions of drifting off, I needed to find out the cause of this dangerous dozing. I was lucky on two occasions, but I was concerned about the possibility of it happening a third time. An accident while dozing was not an option.

I met with my family doctor, Dr. Jon Meier. He wisely thought my first course of action was to have a sleep test. This possibility did not excite me greatly as sleeping away from home was not my most favorite activity, especially when I knew that someone was watching my every move through the monitoring system. I did go on a sleep machine and would encourage others to investigate this possibility if there are any sleep issues. The machine forces air into the body and helps one sleep better. To this date, I use the machine every night of my life.

Special Olympics

State Games

After my retirement in 2006, I was to continue my involvement in Special Olympics in the Meals and Refreshment committee. I finally decided that after forty some years, it was time to let someone else take over the reins. Michele Solether, with the help of my son Mark, continued the program for many years.

Wood County Special Olympics Committee

I had been involved in the Wood County Special Olympics Committee since 1985. When I retired, I continued this involvement and am still involved at the time of the printing of this book. This committee is comprised of parents and others from the community who provide guidance and manpower in areas associated with the Wood County Special Olympics.

One of the changes that has happened more in recent years in Special Olympics is the pairing of Special Olympics athletes with more normal people. A friend of my son Mark's, Scott, was to be paired with a Special Olympics athlete in golf. Scott always relayed to me how much he enjoyed and learned from the Special Olympian in this arrangement. I'm sure the Special Olympian would say the same.

Other Special People

Maggie Hunt

One of the adults in the Wood County program participated with sixty-seven other Ohioans at the National Special Olympics in 2018. Maggie is a high-functioning person and continues to live with her parents. At the national games, Maggie participated in swimming events and received three medals, a bronze in the 100 meter race, a gold in the 4x100 relay, and a gold in the 200 meter. Local coverage on the front page of the *Sentinel-Tribune* paper reported Maggie's accomplishments.

Anne Schooley

I knew Anne through her mother and father, Becky and Carlton Schooley. My wife had been a teacher assigned to Fort Meigs School in

Perrysburg, and Becky was principal for the district. Carlton was also employed as director of transportation for the district. He was also the advisor for our son's fraternity at Bowling Green State University, Sigma Phi Epsilon.

Becky was a Special Olympian in Wood County and participated in the USA Special Olympics Games in Orlando, Florida, in swimming in 2022. This was first on her bucket list of things to do. She earned silver in the 100-meter butterfly, fifth in the 200-meter freestyle, and eighth in the 100-meter freestyle. Great job, Anne.

At a celebrity basketball game, I was talking with Anne's parents when Anne came into the conversation and reminded all that she was the only person in the household who was working out of the home, a nice touch and smile by all happened.

Corey Barnett

One of the responsibilities I assumed for the Special Olympics Advisory Board in Wood County was to be a part of the interview team for a new Special Olympics Coordinator at Wood Lane. In April of 2022, I went to the offices of the Wood County Board of Developmental Disabilities to interview prospects for that position. I went to the door I had been told to enter and found I was not able to enter. Inside, I saw a person cleaning the floor, and he stopped his work and opened the door asking me what I wanted. After telling him I was told to enter this door, he told me I needed to go to another door, and he was not allowed to let me enter for safety reasons.

I went to the other door and was waiting to be escorted to the interview room. Meanwhile, the same person that I had seen vacuuming at the other entrance came to the area I had entered. We started a conversation, and I found the person was a delight to talk with. He informed me that he was a Special Olympian; and he and his brother both participated in flag football, bowling, volleyball, softball, and basketball. I found out his name was Corey Barnett, and we continued a very friendly and enjoyable conversation about the rest of his family. I continued to marvel at the open and friendly conversation that I had with Corey. A man I had known when I was an employee of the board came in, and I assumed it was his supervisor. This supervisor, Tom, joined the conversation; and I caught up with him about his life.

Yes, I found again how social a person with developmental disabilities can be with a complete stranger. It made me feel very good about being involved with Corey and the many other special people I had been able to share my life and theirs with and to share with you, the readers of this book.

Helpful Hints

From time to time, I run across various sayings in e-mails and other written material. One of the sayings that caught my eye came from an unknown author. It said, "Judge your success by what you had to give up in order to get it." There is a lot of truth in this statement, do you agree?

I finished this book in 2023, and the COVID-19 pandemic was still an issue. We lost our son Mark in 2016, and it has never been the same without him. I do have the love of my life, Kathy; my son Joe; and his wife, Tara, and their two sons, Zach and Josh. I hope you have enjoyed this book with the many happenings of a life that was greatly enriched by knowing *Robert and Many Other Special People.*

As I edited this chapter around 6:30 am, I noted a piece of paper found the previous day by my wife. It was from Mark telling me how proud he was of me. What a great way to start my day and end this book!

Printed in the USA
CPSIA information can be obtained
at www.ICGtesting.com
LVHW061246071023
760211LV00003B/458